i am rev

magda lopez

i am rev

Magda Lopez

ISBN: 978-1-09837-010-7

i have O.C.D.

i am rev.

Rev means /rev/

noun

noun: rev; plural noun: revs

a revolution of an engine per minute.

"an engine speed of 1,750 revs"

an act of increasing the speed of revolution of a vehicle's engine by pressing the accelerator, especially while the clutch is disengaged.

"she started it up with a violent rev of the engine"

verb

verb: rev; 3rd person present: revs; past tense: revved; past participle: revved; gerund or present participle: revving

increase the running speed of (an engine) or the engine speed of (a vehicle) by pressing the accelerator, especially while the clutch is disengaged.

"he got into the car, revved up the engine and drove off"

(of an engine or vehicle) operate with increasing speed when the accelerator is pressed, especially while the clutch is disengaged.

"he could hear the sound of an engine revving nearby"

make or become more active or energetic.

"he's revving up for next week's World Cup game"

Origin

early 20th century: **abbreviation of revolution.**

Secret: People call me Rev more than they call me Mag.

CHAPTER 2

i am grateful.

The dedication of this book is incredibly special. This book is dedicated to a writer, dedicated to a journalist, dedicated to a screenplay director, dedicated to a poet, dedicated to a movie producer, dedicated to an actor, dedicated to the first Cuban talk show host in New York City, dedicated to a legendary Miami radio personality, dedicated to a ferocious protector, dedicated to an honorary Interpol sharpshooter, dedicated to my father. He is always in my heart. His mellifluous voice is always in my ear, and his strong presence is always in the mirror staring back at me. THANK GOD! I love you Papi.

**Secret: If you Google "ENRIQUE DE LA TORRE,"
you will be impressed, I promise.**

i am going to live forever.

My name is Magda de la Torre Lopez, AKA @REVETE. If I get married again, I will change my last name again. I believe in marriage still. I am human. I bleed just like you. I know this book is going to be criticized. I know it is not going to be accepted by everyone, and that is okay by me. What's new, pussy cat? I know I am going to hurt people's feelings. That is not the intention. I am not for everyone. Criticism is something that I learn from. Feedback is power. When I wake up every morning, my goal is not to make people happy. My goal is to always maintain my own happiness first. That goal is sometimes overwhelming. It is a full-time job.

I am writing this book because I needed to write this book. It is a story of survival. For many years, I wondered how on earth I made it, how I got through it. As an unsupervised child, my main source of defense was developing habits. Also, developing O.C.D. I can remember this process all the way back to pre-teen years. I always ask my clients to describe their day from the moment they open their eyes. 'Oh, I am a CERTIFIED life coach, did I forget to mention this?" It is in the daily habits that you can identify EVERYTHING. I believe that this strength of developing positive habits was one of my strongest defense mechanisms. Also, my business. I turned it into a business. What else do you do with lemons?

This book is not meant to hurt anyone or insult anyone. I apologize in advance if it does. On the contrary, it is meant as a form of therapy for me, and the result of many years of wondering if my story could help another human being. My story is not different from other people's stories. I just have the courage and the sticktoitiveness to tell it. We all suffer pain and love loss.

Hopefully, through my pain you can move. We all do not have the deep need to share our pain. And that is okay too. I have never walked a day in your shoes. But I hope that after reading parts of my life (the juicy ones), you will share yours in your own way at your own time. It is my hope that you gain some confidence, laugh out loud, and grow your knowledge. It is my goal to share some true insight into who MAGDA really is. She is vastly different than @REVETE.

Grab some popcorn, this is one hell of a ride.

Secret: Originally, I was afraid to get on social media for fear of privacy issues. HA! HA! HA!

CHAPTER 4

i am cuban.

Growing up in Miami means being a Cuban patriot. Trust me, bro, you don't have a choice. I was born in the United States but felt like a Cuban patriot all my life. In my high school history class, my essays were always on Cuba. It is what I knew. In Sociology, my observations were always about Fidel Castro and the demise of Cuba. I had no choice but to defend my country even if it was their country.

My father was not only a patriot, but he was also a hardcore Batistiano. My father died defending his country on air and every other way possible. I knew he would never live to see a free Cuba. I had lost interest in meeting Cuba after he died. He would always tell me about how he was going to introduce me to his birthplace and show me my heritage and los tinajones de Camaguey. I knew it wouldn't happen, not in his lifetime.

My father fought communism with his microphone on television and radio for over fifty years. His interpretation on how to attack Fidel was effective. His name was placed on a list of Cuban immigrants that weren't allowed back into the island. Fidel had active connections in Miami as well. My father would receive death threats, bomb threats, and all kinds of rhetoric because he exercised his right to freedom of speech.

He was fortunate enough to make a healthy living using his heart-driven passion in defense of his country.

My mother described her adjustment issues in school after she arrived in Miami Beach. She came at a much younger age than my father. Her concerns were less political. They both remember a beautiful island and its fond memories.

As a child of Cuban immigrants living in Miami, it is hard to remember that we lived in the United States. Miami, for all my life, has been a tiny Cuba. I can choose a myriad of places in Miami that are made to mimic and replicate different parts of Cuba.

The Cubans that came to America at the time my parents did worked quickly and diligently to recreate their lives–or create something as close to their lives as possible. They rebuilt the same restaurants, i.e. Versailles, Casa Larios, El Pub, etc.

The radio stations were also duplicated CMQ, WQBA, and others. The Calle Ocho parade was my father's playground. Anyone who loved and defended Cuba would gather there annually to celebrate Cuba. The slamming of the dominoes, the smoking of the Cohiba cigars, and the sounds of Celia Cruz are a typical day anywhere in Miami.

When I moved to Canada during my developmental years, the thing I missed the most was Cuban coffee (Café Bustelo) and platanos maduros. I remember being in Toronto and longing to taste these tastes again. I can't imagine how the Cuban population felt and still feels about having to abandon everything they knew. All the fucking feels.

I was never privy to Fidel and his bullshit regime–I am second generation– but man, did I ever want to kill him. He stole so much from so many. Every time the news reported the failing of his health, I took out my pots and pans to celebrate. I wish my father could've rejoiced in this celebration.

In my house today, you can find mementos of Cuba throughout. I feel very Cuban even though I own an American passport.

After my father died, I felt there was nothing left for me to see in Cuba. My mother's family was nonexistent in Cuba by the year 2000. The architecture was decayed. Where would I go? What would I see? I decided to kiss that dream away and add Fiji to my bucket list. I made a choice to live vicariously through photographs, stories, and the new Cuba called Miami to keep that dream alive. When I speak of Cuba, most people believe I was born there. The passion coming through the lens of my parents comes through me vividly. I learned the ABCs at the same time I learned about El Malecon. I learned my 123s and about La Virgen de La Caridad simultaneously, too.

I remember sharing a story of my maternal grandmother flying to Cuba to rescue family jewels with my neighbor and adopted sister Mimi. I would tell Mimi all the Cuban stories often. She would share her Lebanese stories. The suffering was the same, the places were different. The loss was heart-wrenching and unanimous.

My grandmother was a seamstress and stay-at-home wife and mother. She was an innocent American. She filed a 1040 tax return as a spouse. She had no real experience with infiltrating countries, spy-like activity and theft. She and the other families that were close to ours in Miami chose her to rescue the treasure because she was the least likely to get caught.

She sewed herself a custom trench coat with the lining removed and flew back to Cuba on a mission. She went to our family home with the mission of saving everyone's jewelry and treasure. This included deeds to properties, wills, photographs, and some of the rarest stones I had ever seen. The relatives of the immigrants that had left Cuba joined forces and kept hiding all of this in order for someone from Miami to come and save it eventually.

One of these families was the Bacardi family. The Bacardi family owns the Cuban rum, and our families were close for many generations. When my grandmother arrived in Cuba, she found the specific tile in the floor that had secretly hidden all these treasures for all of these years. She cracked it open and began sewing the treasures into the coat. The coat was approximately forty pounds heavy when she was done.

My grandmother was about 5'3 and weighs approximately 130 lbs. Flying back to Miami in 85 degree weather with this coat on was going to be a daunting task. She did it anyway.

Can you imagine this little Abuelita coming through the airport with millions of dollars on her body? She was carrying many heirlooms for many families. I remember her almost fainting when she arrived at her Coral Gables casita. I also remember all the Cuban families coming to touch their history once again. The love was priceless. The pain was moving. The tears were endless. My grandmother accomplished a MISSION IMPOSSIBLE with this heroic act.

Mimi would almost cry listening to me tell my Cuban tales. Actually, recant their tales. These stories weren't even mine. They felt like mine. I felt them in my core, in my heart and genuinely as if they had happened to me. I am a patriot.

On my 48th birthday, Mimi gave me the most incredible birthday gift: a plane ticket to Cuba. I cried. I contemplated not going. Was I betraying my father? Was I forfeiting all the Cubans in Miami? Was I a traitor? Cuba was the number one destination for travel in Canada for many years. It used to make me sick to hear people exploiting what was left of Cuba for cheap travel purposes. I swore I would never go back until the country was free. It was a free country on my 48th birthday. Why was I having so many mind blocks and guilt about going to Cuba? The struggle was real. After a long discussion with my son about whether I should go, I decided to accept the gift. Was my name on the list of "NOT WELCOME IN CUBA?" I am my father's daughter. I changed my last name for marriage. Did the communist government do that to me too? All these thoughts were front and center when I got on that plane headed towards Havana.

We stayed in the Kuwaiti embassy. This mansion was in the most horrific condition. It was palatial. It was awe-inspiring. The doors, hinges, knobs, and layout were an architect's dream. The landscaping and pool were built for kings. I felt so guilty staying there. I knew the country was poverty-stricken and here I was, betraying everything I lived as a child for a birthday celebration in the lap of luxury. I had to breathe deeply throughout this trip because there were several moments where I was overcome with guilt for the suffering of all the Cubans.

Our mansion shared property lines with the U.S. Embassy. One of the people in our group made me pee laughing in the Olympic sized pool on this trip because he kept saying things like, "If anything happens, we'll just jump the fence from this embassy to the United States embassy and be safe." I spoke a lot to the chauffeurs, cleaning staff, and cooks. Mimi did everything she could to celebrate my birthday and I was incredibly grateful, but the silent battle I had in my interior was real AF. We had food prepared for us daily, the best of the best. I felt guilt and sadness. There was nothing really to enjoy outside of the company I was in because there is NOTHING left in Cuba. It is a ruined country.

We went to an art gallery and I cried again. There were many happy tears and many sad ones, too. Mimi gave me a timeless gift. She gave me the courage to see what I felt. She brought me closer to all the deceased people in my life waiting for their country to be free. She gave me closure and hope all at the same time. I rushed back to Miami to record the "represent" podcast on Cuba and my experience. "Oh, I have a podcast, it's the MAGDA LOPEZ PODCAST, did I forget to mention this too?" I didn't want to miss a thing. I needed to memorialize all of it.

It is an interesting podcast from my perspective. It's an account of an American citizen, more patriotic than a Cuban-born immigrant, invited to the island by a Lebanese immigrant born in Paris and vacationing in a Kuwaiti embassy. Y QUE VIVA CHANGO!!!!! Some Cubans believe in CHANGO a mighty Santeria warrior.

My trainer Grant always asks me where I'm from. Some days I'm Canadian, some days I'm American, some days I'm Greek, and some days I'm Jewish. But every fucking damn day, SOY CUBANA!!!!

Secret: Madonna's first child is Cuban.

CHAPTER 5

i am a daughter.

I spent my younger life in a Miami radio station, many Miami radio stations. WQBA AM La Cubanisima, the sister station to SUPER Q, was the shit! The theme song was "SUPER Q, I LOVE YOU, La mejor musica la tocas tu." My father's show was *DESDE MI TORRE por Enrique de la Torre.*

My maiden name means of the tower. Magda Antonia of the Tower. My mother's maiden name was Magda Lopez. My name now is Magda Lopez. What can you tell about someone by their name? I think a name can govern who you become. I grew up in front of a Miami camera, many cameras. I grew up in front of an audience. I was always wonderfully comfortable in that environment. It did not matter what he did for a living, I felt comfortable in front of an audience. He was my father. I adored him. He was a fierce protector. He loved me unconditionally. It was fine, the cameras, the microphones, the people—nothing could touch me. I truly felt protected next to my father. Obsessed with this feeling, by the way.

I would smile at everyone. This is where I believe I perfected the smile variations. I would talk to everyone. I think my father was shocked as to how outgoing I was. I would roll with the public punches, watch, and learn. He was friends with the coolest cats: my favorite was Walter Mercado, for sure. My genius editor thinks this is a cool fact. I agree with her. Walter must be the best-dressed astrologist in the history of mankind.

My father's voice and presence competed with the best. The radio business is viciously competitive. In Spanish, he was part of the FARANDULA, or celebrity, and by default, so was I. He was one of the "10 GALANES de CUBA," or top ten best-looking Cuban men in the entertainment business. For me, he was just my dad. I would watch him put on his makeup and fix his hair. He dressed for the part, too. He was a consummate actor. I do not ever remember feeling shy or awkward in this light. I was a little girl in Miami watching the influx of Cubans adore my father, a freedom fighter. The parades on Calle Ocho were awesome memories. He would sit me down next to him and I would stare and wave at all his fans. He was kind of Elvis-like. He was one the few Cuban immigrants who could voice what all the Cubans in Miami felt and get paid for it.

This privilege did not come without a price. I also watched as he suffered death threats, bomb threats, and all kinds of controversy. Fidel had reach in Miami, too. My father would report remotely from all the riots in Miami. His lime green Cadillac was always packed with guns—he always carried five on his body. He would've been a great bounty hunter. The car was as long as a small Intrepid boat; how my dad parked that sucker; I will never know.

I cried when he went to the Rodney King riots. I prayed. Anytime you are telling a story, people will not agree, people will criticize you, and some people will retaliate. Cheers to freedom of speech. He was accustomed to this and always at the ready. The bullets and viciousness that came from his business, his purpose, and his passion ricocheted like boomerangs. I learned a lot from this. His ability to do his work and not honor the crap, the noise, and the negativity was admirable. He was extremely approachable and highly guarded at the same time. I am that way exactly. This lesson will forever be one of my favorites.

Flash forward twenty years. I got an opportunity to work on the radio. I turned it down; my ex-husband and his antics got in the way of that dream. I had a great chance and I declined it. It was maybe one of the biggest professional mistakes I ever made in my life. I was offered a part-time job paying six figures to work in what I knew. Back when radio was radio— we are talking about close to thirty years ago—this was the role of a lifetime. I should have said yes. It would have changed my life. But being cheated on and being in the public eye do not mix well. My ex-husband knew that. I would have found out he was unfaithful sooner. I passed up on a great professional career. I desperately wanted to accept it. I wanted to be on the air. I wanted to be just like my dad. I feel like I was born with that talent. I regret rejecting this deeply.

Podcasts were born. Radio stopped being the journalistic format it used to be. Radio personalities were no longer earning the salaries my father earned. Joe Rogan is a maverick. Essentially, the internet killed the radio star. Thank God my father was not alive to watch the slow death of radio. But I had a little money left from my divorce, so I bought my podcast equipment. I do not know what the fuck I am doing. I grew up in radio, not podcasts!

No one knows what they are doing, really. I launch the Magda Lopez Podcast. I can be heard on iTunes, Spotify, iHeartMedia, and countless other platforms. I record, edit, and upload content all by myself. I still do not know what I am doing. The commercial spots come. The interviews come. The money comes. I still do not know what I am doing. I am creating lead sheets, legacy, and history, and have no clue what I am doing. I love to meet people that act like they know what they are doing. However, I am consistent, just like my father. His beacon score was the highest I ever saw. I still do not know what I am doing, but what I do know is I have a voice, a following. I am funny, and I can drive people. I have an opinion. I am @REVETE. This must count for something, right?

Advertising makes money. Marketing makes money. Talent is expensive. I have got everything it takes to hang with Joe Rogan and Gary Vee. I do not know enough about the tech world of podcasting to know where else the podcast is being heard, but I know I am out there in places that I've never even heard of. What I do know for certain is that I have created a seven-and-a-half-year show on my own, all while not knowing what the fuck I am doing. I have listeners, haters, and fans, and I have ratings and insights. I am so grateful. Where this show goes, I do not know. Anything is possible.

I do not know if I began the podcast because I wanted to be close to my dad. Or if I simply wanted to lift my voice and tell my story, all stories. I do not know if I grabbed the mic and originated the show because I passed up on that opportunity in my twenties. I do not know if I continued the show because I met a young man named Mike Gregory. I do not know why, but I know that the podcast has been consistent, just like everything about me and my dad. My dad and I were a tiny little gang. I think consistency is sexy. If you have not heard my show, I want you to hear it. Feedback is power.

When I turn on the mic, my voice changes. It is not a natural voice. My father's voice, though, was natural, a gorgeous, unmistakable voice. Simply perfect! He sounded like Mufasa in *The Lion King*. James Earl Jones and my father must have been related in a previous life. He knew how to make people laugh. He knew how to make people cry. He knew how to write, edit, and record in one take. The man was so gifted. He earned a living on the microphone in a country where he did not speak the language. I am so proud of him and his talent. His eyes so blue.

I do not think I am as talented as he was. I really do not. But I am more fearless than he ever was. He knew it, too. He taught me how to defend myself. He taught me how to channel my O.C.D, which he had, too. He aimed to kill. He was a sharpshooter and an honorary member of the INTERPOL. Like him, I love guns. Whenever I go to the fair or have a gun in hand, I win. My father and I spent a lot of time shooting together. I call my current love "my shooter" for different reasons. My father was the OG shooter in my life. "OG" means original gangsta.

If you Google my father, he is there. A star. Which is impressive, considering he would be 110 years old now. My father was married five times. The man was a stone-cold fox and a rolling stone. He had one child: *ME*. He had one grandchild: *ROMAN*. If he were alive today, things would be hugely different for me. He inspired my mic life, and he would have been immensely proud of this.

My father's daughter could do no wrong. I loved that about him. Isn't that what love is: protecting the ones you love from everything and everyone, always? I do not know where my mic life is going. Your feedback is crucial to me, help a sista out. I bought my own mic. He was given his. My father's life "on air" lasted for more than fifty years. His shows were conventional; predictable and safe. He was this way, too. My show is unconventional and unpredictable. I am that way. What I share with my father is that we both said exactly what we wanted to say fearlessly. He did not even know about Howard Stern back then. He reminds me of Howard in many ways.

Secret: Say what you need to say.

CHAPTER 6

I am a mom.

There is no such thing as a perfect parent. Parents do the best they can with the tools they have. This is the belief that got me through my childhood, and the belief that I applied as a parent myself.

I finally got pregnant after four years of trying. If your husband is spreading his semen across the city, you are lucky to grab some for yourself. I promised my baby I would never hit him. I promised him I would protect him from all evil. I promised him I would nurture him with all my tools. Luckily for him, my chest of tools was big. I had grabbed all the useful ones throughout my life and kept them in storage for him. MAGDA the BUILDER was working.

I honored my promises to my son, and I made another promise to my father on his death bed. As he was seconds away from dying, my father asked me to "never leave Roman alone." I acquiesced. It was a life sentence making that promise. It was having to host all events, all play dates, all sleepovers. It was a *stop living and just be a parent* command. It was *forget my name and stand outside of Roman's classroom for a dozen years to make sure no one touches him*. I did that. I honored my promise to my father. I still do.

The first time I was sexually violated I was eight years old. My mother was one wall away from me while it was happening. It was the little brother of her best friend. I was raped for the first time when I was thirteen, an Italian guy in Canada. My mother was working, and I was left in the care of my rapist. Who the fuck leaves a teenage girl in the care of a 28-year-old man? I mentally blocked the rest of the sexual assaults after that. There were too many to count.

I cannot remember the first time I was physically abused. I do not remember not being physically abused, ever. The last time I was hit by my mother, I was seventeen years old. I never lived in her home again after that final beating.

There are adults that can testify to this, but I do not care if they do or do not. I can testify to this.

It took me forty years to speak of this to my mother directly. She did not apologize. She tried to justify it all. There is NO justification for physically harming a child. EVER.

I never understood what or why this happened to me, or to anyone, really. Why would someone have a child only to harm them? I WAS A DEVIL CHILD. I was always in trouble. I also was a stellar over-achiever. On both counts, I was desperately seeking her approval and love. I wanted the pain to stop so I did everything I could to get her attention. Instead of receiving what I was looking for, I got a shoe in the lip. A protractor in the back. A backhand across my face. Over and over and over again.

There were the beatings in public. I still remember people trying to save me. I remember the people that tried to stop her. I remember hoping they could. They never could. She was my mother. If you were one of those people that tried to help me, thank you.

My father tried to stop the abuse various times, but he was limited because of distance. My parents were divorced when I was two years old. I was born in New Jersey and they lived in Queens, New York until the divorce. I am a JERSEY GIRL. Childbirth was free for television stars. She was thirty years younger than he was—I told you he was a fox. He was married five times, but he ONLY loved her. She was the only woman he had a child with.

I can't imagine one day in a house with those two humans as husband and wife—you are talking about two atomic bombs. The passion must have been mind-blowing. My mother once tried to discuss sex with my father with me, and I remember feeling sick. Like, barf city sick. She tried to be my friend a lot. This also made me kind of sick. How can you be friends with someone you do not trust?

My mother failed to recognize that the abuse created fear in me in every way. When a child is born, they have no choice but to trust their caregivers. My first caregiver was my mother. My first opportunity to trust was shattered by abuse. Her coping mechanism was hitting me. She had an enormous amount of stress, but she brought this stress on herself. Her election to be a professional income earner was the main source of stress. She chose this because she wanted it. I was proud of her then and am proud of her now. I applaud women that go into the workforce and trailblaze. But in this process, she lost all interest in motherhood and I learned how to run an office and survive with what I could. I also learned what not to do in my future as a parent. I am eternally grateful for these lessons, despite how scarring they were.

Roman won. My son inevitably won. I was not given a book on how to parent; I just remembered what not to do. I fed him three times a day. I did homework with him daily. I was the room parent for all his life. I became furniture in his school. I respected his body. For God's sake, I made his body. I led all events. I did everything my mother never did, and it worked like magic. The idea of striking my son physically is paralyzing. My ex-husband never hit our son either. He knew I would have to bite him again. He knew better.

Being a parent is the hardest job any adult could have. It is also the highest privilege anyone can be awarded.

I just called Roman and reminded him to charge his phone. He is in Baltimore, rescuing his storage items from college. He is currently five months away from being 21 years old. He and I are tight on the LIFE360 app. His response is, "You're crazy, Mom." He is right, but I am also at peace knowing he is safe and locatable. I was thirteen and getting sexually abused with my mothers' consent by a married man. Call me crazy all you want; I am okay with that kind of crazy.

I work out hard. I am so driven that sometimes I scare myself. There are times I feel my arms and quads get too thick. I know who I am hitting. I know why I do this. I am still fighting back. I am punching back. I am defending myself. It is the healthiest way to win. I keep these thoughts to myself. I harness them and work. I always feel better afterwards.

When my ex-husband's fist grazed my cheek on that dreaded day—the day I became a Sug Knight, you know, the rapper—I remembered being abused as a child. I remembered losing my marriage to worthless sex with countless employees and baseball moms and whoever else he could find. I remembered losing my father. I remembered I had Roman to protect. The Incredible Hulk came alive.

I still feel weird when another human comes near me physically. I only touch my son to hug him or kiss his head. I am incredibly careful with him. He is my baby. Children love me. They gravitate towards me. I often wonder if they can feel I was abused, if they can feel my fears. I work with children as often as I can. It is my way of healing. I speak to children in adult terms. They understand. I only use baby talk with my boyfriend. He understands.

I speak at schools, teach yoga in homeless shelters, serve in church, spend as much time with children as I possibly can. They are the future. They are our hope for a better world.

If I saw a child getting hit, I would probably go to jail again. I have a weakness for the elderly and children. They are innocent. They must be protected. This desire to fix situations has not always been beneficial to me. I would not change it ever.

When people ask me about my mother, I smile like the Cheshire cat in *Alice in Wonderland* and say she is well. I do not discuss my upbringing with reference to her. I leave it out. It is not that I am embarrassed about it. It is what it is. I just hate sympathy. I have too much to do in the world. I have too much to give and create.

Dwelling on what could have been is a sad place to be. I do not do sad well, or for lengthy amounts of time. I miss the dead, of course. I ONLY fear health issues—and lizards.

My mother and I have no relationship. I ended it approximately four years ago. Abuse began in other ways. Unlike my father, she did not defend me at all costs as a child and then as an adult. I will never understand that.

If Roman killed someone, I mean murdered another human being, I would defend him. He is my son. I made him a promise when he was born, and I intend to keep it until I die. I do not give a shit what the circumstances are: when you bring children into this world it is a lifetime commitment to love, protect, and nurture them, first and forever. This is my belief, and I am entitled to it.

My mother taught me how to dance. My mother taught me how to survive at all costs. My mother is a highly creative woman. I forgave my mother a long time ago, and I pray that she is happy with her life and the people in it. I made a gift to myself in doing this. I chose not to allow any type of further abuse by her or anyone else EVER again.

I did not want to write this chapter. I did not want to hurt her further. I cannot imagine what it would feel like to have a child and a grandchild and have no contact with them. After reading the first draft of this book together with my attorneys, I realized this is an urgent part of my life that was the catalyst for the rest of the glorious moments, and it had to be memorialized. I also needed to share where I come from without bias or prejudice and in complete transparency.

I DO NOT JUDGE my mother, I THANK her. She did the best she could with the tools in her box. I still put my hands up in defense any time someone comes near me. When my acupuncturist asked me if I had ever been abused, I was shocked. He said he could tell in my muscles. I have an extremely difficult time in personal relationships. I trust very few people. If you touch me in an incorrect way or without warning, DUCK! This is the PTSD left over in me. I work on it daily, and this book has been cathartic. I am certain I will be working on this process of self-love for the rest of my life. It is a never-ending journey, parenting.

**Secret: Now, you know why I own the Steel
Mace practice. #mommydearest**

CHAPTER 7

i am powerful.

This morning, my girlfriend and sister and fellow Instagram mover Sara Quiriconi messaged me. She sent a brief description of me and included the words, "Magda is a powerhouse." I laughed out loud. I laughed hard. I rarely laugh out loud. I really hate when people use "LOL," too. It takes a funny person or statement for me to laugh out loud, and I believe very few people are funny. But Sara made me laugh hard. I don't see myself as powerful. I see myself as powerless. I see myself as always trying to take my power back.

I knew I was different as a child. I knew there were habits in my life that were unusual. I didn't know why though. It took years of visiting many counselors and therapists for me to learn why I was different. I kept hearing O.C.D. and not understanding what that was or how I got it. Did someone pass this on to me? Was I born with this? What is O.C.D.?

I would make lists. I still make lists. I have lists for everything. I write it all down. I have all the devices, but I only trust my handwriting. I know it's mine and no one is tricking me. I have an intense fear of lies. I reorganize all things repeatedly and have done this for as long as I can remember. I repeat myself verbally. I do this out loud and silently.

I must sit in the same place and do the same things, or I feel out of place. I eat the same foods and never mix them on the plate. If I can't visually identify the foods I am eating, I won't eat. I need to use the same instruments or feel out of control. I feel cleaning and cooking are necessary to be clean-clean in the mind.

I trust very few people. I have an extremely hard time letting people into my world. I become afraid if someone touches me without an invitation. I try hard not to make eye contact. These are habits and rituals I have practiced for as long as I can remember. I am paranoid. I call it heightened awareness, but clearly know it is paranoia.

I used to think I had a disease. I did. It is not self-diagnosed. It is not Jack Nicholson mumbo jumbo. It is a small and protected bubble I live in. I love my bubble.

What is remarkable about this is I am extremely public and very social. I am notorious for being the life of the party. I am also known for making an appearance and sneaking out the back door. I can't do the public thing for too long. I have learned there is a time limit. I begin to get itchy if left out in the vulnerable world for too long. I am an oxymoron.

My son asked me to include this chapter because he feels it is a big part of me. And like me, he loves to help others. He, too, is an empath. He wholeheartedly felt that if I wrote a chapter on this, it might help someone else. I agreed with him. My genius editor agrees with my son too.

I am not embarrassed about having O.C.D.—I am proud of it. I think defects are beautiful, but also, I don't see having this disease as a defect. I see it as an asset. About 2.3 percent of people suffer from O.C.D. at one point their lifetime. I didn't know what I had or why I had it, but I used it to my advantage.

I won awards for being first at everything. I won votes because of it, too. I am a project smasher. I crush all goals I set for myself. This isn't free. I lose sleep, health, and money all the time. Winning isn't the goal; I use my O.C.D. as a form of completion and control. Loose ends make me nervous. I harnessed these peculiar habits and behaviors in my favor.

These habits became my defense mechanism. I didn't have traditional parents, but I had great accomplishments. I didn't have a husband who only loved me, but I had a son who was my best friend. I used all my losses as methods to achieve. I controlled what was in my control. I defended myself.

As an older human, I began to educate myself on where this came from. There is no one gene that can be attributed to the development of O.C.D., a chronic mental illness, but I learned the number one source of O.C.D. is child abuse. BAM! I solved the mystery. No D.N.A. proof needed. I never took medicine for my O.C.D., by the way. I don't take medicine unless I have to.

I remember my son developing a blinking issue when my ex-husband and I began fighting in court. He had never displayed this tic until then. It breaks my heart remembering his beautiful eyes reacting to stress. I wish I could've spoken to my ex-husband about this, but it wouldn't have helped. He probably would've sued me again. Thankfully, my son overcame this habit.

I, however, never stopped writing lists, checking locks, repeating acts incessantly and protecting myself from the world. I have a physical activity I do whenever I find myself under stress: my hands go up. It's almost like I'm ready to strike. I suppose getting hit often and never knowing when it was going to happen taught me this.

I have an intense fear of lizards. My father always used to try to talk me through this phobia, but his words meant nothing. I can't be near a lizard. The fear is crippling.

Many people who know me see me as an extraordinary achiever—a powerhouse, like Sara said. This couldn't be farther from the truth. I use many techniques developed at an early age to grip power for life. I leave everything early—like, ridiculously early. I lay out my clothes daily. I am a hoarder. I have an extreme fear of not having enough.

Sharing this information is not scary at all. I was shocked when Roman told me he thought this would be useful, but I thought about it for a while and saw his logic. I believe that pain is my friend, just like O.C.D.. O.C.D. was my partner through all the madness. Every time I suffered physical or sexual abuse, I cleaned and organized everything a lot. When I found out my marriage was a fraud, I made lists. I felt better about my world ending. It's absurd, and yet made perfect sense. In chaos, I found clarity, always.

Every time I landed in another home as a child, I would sit quietly observe and listen. I would learn their habits, customs, and language. I would grow through the pain of not having my own home. It would fuel my need to succeed in other ways.

Embracing the anxiety, stress, fear and transforming it in my favor has been one of my best superpowers. Becoming a coach was profitable because, through the trust I earned from companies and the people in them, I was able to heal myself. This privilege of trust empowered me to do more. I became a bigger philanthropist. People sought me out in times of need both personally and professionally—I was honorable. I suppose this is power.

I'm always amazed by what people voluntarily tell me. I guess they see me as tangible, human—imperfect. I know this is power.

If I had had a normal upbringing and a healthy marriage, I maybe would've been a deserving asshole. Instead, I became a person for the people. My soul bleeds for people. I give more than I take. This hasn't worked in my favor. It doesn't matter. When I die, I'm dying in peace. I'm not afraid of having my heart broken. I'm not afraid of taking chances or risks. There is nothing I can't bounce back from. O.C.D. has taught me this. It has been my strongest ally. It is like the cigarettes: always with me. I trust my O.C.D. to always help me overcome and then succeed.

**Secret: If powerful is having a chronic mental
illness, then YES! I am a powerhouse.**

CHAPTER 8

i was blair warner.

I remember feeling scared when I arrived at The Bethany Hills School. It was picturesque. The grounds were manicured and the buildings where we would live were brand new.

I think we were the original housewives of The Bethany Hills School. We were a group of girls living in an all-girls' boarding school, growing through life as a team. Mr. Glover, our history teacher, called us rabble rousers. I still have no idea what that meant. Ms. Drummond was the coolest art teacher any student could dream of; Chiaroscuro is a lesson I will never forget. My cheerleading coach was from Michigan and made the squad's creation a challenge. I *crushed* that. I bruised my inner thighs like a champ landing in a straddle split. I made it!!

For me, boarding school was a very welcome break. I was able to be a child. The time I spent in this school gave me irreplaceable life lessons. I learned how to speak English there. The English in Miami is quite different than the one in Canada: it's more of a dialect. I learned French at Bethany, too. The girls in our school were there for each other when no one else was. We were family.

We ate three meals a day in the dining hall together. We prayed together, although it was a non-denominational school. We cried together; many breakups were shared here. We got in trouble together. We succeeded together. We failed together. It was the safest time in my life. I had supervision and was cared for. The school was awfully expensive, but worth every penny.

It was located in the town of Bethany, Ontario. There were five hundred and five people in this place. The girls in uniform were notorious, glamourous, and unmistakable. Think Zsa Zsa in Green Acres. I loved wearing a uniform. I wore makeup; I did my hair. I also wore zit cream and grew fat like a tomato. I ate like it was going out of style. It was cold AF.

Some of the girls were dropped off in helicopters, limousines, and chauffeur-driven vehicles. I was extremely poor compared to my peers. My mother dropped me off, all while reminding me how much of a financial burden I was.

We made memories for life. I was one of three Spanish-speaking girls on campus. We had girls from all over the world in this school.

For physical education, we rode horses and skied. I became an aggressive hockey player. Ice-skating is a whole other world compared to the Miami roller-skating days. I was dominant at Hot Wheels but had to start from scratch on the ice. They rode horses at Bethany, I clapped for them. We were an equestrian school. I am terrified of horses. We had the best-looking cheer squad I ever saw. And there was Bethany government. Of course, I ended up in government, along with my chosen friends. It is not a coincidence that my friends and I took over the school government. We were leaders back then and leaders now. I remember the day of the election when the Head Mistress called our names as the winners. What a glorious day!

The girls in our school became prominent lawyers, entrepreneurs, and creatives. (I guess we can add author to that list now!) I can go anywhere in the world, and one of our Bethany sisters is there, crushing life. It is a great feeling.

My parents sacrificed a lot sending me to this school. I am eternally grateful they did. I cannot think of a more peaceful time in my life.

Since leaving the school, I have had the privilege of going to weddings, reunions, and events with my Bethany sisters. I have met their children and families. Two of our sisters have died. One committed suicide. Rest in peace, Sandra Bennett.

The fabric that was woven in this school will forever live on. The life connections have had a funny way of coming around again. I mention a few of these ladies in the chapter titled "I am lucky," and I am indeed lucky. We are at an age where funerals are prevalent and travel is available. I am an only child but believe I have at least fifty sisters in this world. We are eternally BHS girls. It is a tie that will forever bind.

It was not always easy; girls can be mean. There was mean girls too, but few.

When I say I went to boarding school, people look at me funny. They think I was not loved or maybe a troubled child. I was both things. However, the time I spent in The Bethany Hills School was even better than the *Facts of Life* television show. It was bliss. No one abused me there; no one lied to me there. I was able to be a child with supervision. I really wanted to know what that felt like. I was truly fortunate for these years.

My role in our school was yearbook, senior soccer, Social Head, cheerleader, Red Rope wearer (only four of us had them), and forever troublemaker.

If I could pick a character in *Facts of Life* that I resembled in personality, it would be Blair. Big hair, stylish, and overachieving was my modus operandi.

Secret: I had two dates for every formal. I was always a lover.

CHAPTER 9

i am loyal.

Meryl Streep and Dustin Hoffman made a movie called *Kramer vs. Kramer*. I do not know how old you are, but this movie is timeless. As a matter of fact, I have decided to watch it again after I write this chapter. #NOSTALGIC.

This movie rips at your heartstrings. It is a vein splitter, a movie of divorce. Anytime a love union ends in a court battle, it's tragedy.

My last ten years were a pseudo-movie based on divorce. This movie includes many shady attorneys, one judge that hated me, and many Miami professionals. My rap sheet, thanks to the past ten years of my life, makes 2Chainz look docile.

When I said yes to marrying my husband and accepted his ring(s), I never in my life imagined that I would go through this torturous process called divorce. I never expected to live through my own tragic movie scene.

It has been a challenge to continue being happy, creating and living under the pressure of being attacked constantly. My former husband remains bitter with me and is currently married for the third time. I wish he would focus more on his wife than on me. He's angry: *how could I have left him? Why didn't I just stay and keep quiet like all the other wives?* But who the fuck knowingly stays in an adulterous marriage? I cannot judge what others do, but I can promise you that I will NEVER agree to being lied to.

I lacked the traditional, conventional family unit as a child. I urgently longed for a happy marriage. I wanted the perfect scenario, but there is no such thing as a perfect anything. However, there is a boundary I set when I agreed to marry him, and it was a simple one: *it's just you and me against the world.* It is all I ever wanted. I never wanted to be an entrepreneur or an income earner; I wanted to be a mother and a housewife. Life took turns and twists I was ill-prepared for, and ultimately, it was him and the world against me. He slept with many women over a course of twenty years. He conspired against me in ways other than the sexual. It was diabolical.

I knew at an incredibly young age what my boundaries were, regarding marriage. He was supposed to be my BEST FRIEND. He was supposed to be my PROTECTOR. But this did not happen the way I thought it would have, and a third person in any relationship is a dealbreaker. I knew it then, and I die by this belief now.

I was devastated when I found out. I was an alien to myself. I could not recognize what was real anymore. I was not angry—I was hurt.

Anger has a boomerang effect. I believe that when you get angry at someone, it kills you. It is a boomerang. It is a Boomeranger. I took time to understand the situation I was placed in and then, I acted. I was not angry. I am not angry now. It took every ounce of courage for me to smile, function, and live. Still, I remained happy.

What happened to me happens too often. Most people dwell and stay in anger. Most people try to fix the unfixable. I know myself. I could not do it. I could not sweep it under the rug. Happy is the goal, with or without the pipe dream. With or without a husband.

In the movie *Kramer vs. Kramer*, the couple ends up agreeing on child custody. In my divorce, we have yet to agree on anything. It is my wish that all the (too many) people involved in the demise of my marriage be happy and healthy for eternity. I wish all haters love and light.

I have better things to do. I love to work. I love to generate. I love to create. I am a miracle in motion. I am a work in progress.

Turning my script into a true love story took HUTZPA! I decided to take this tragic storyline and fall in love with life again. I decided to fall in love with the unconventional family. It was me and Roman against all odds. He was Sonic and I was Tails. I made the mental shift of living instead of dying. I learned to step out of the childhood aspirations and expectations and successfully slapped O.C.D. in the face. I quit smoking; I became strong. I did take a ride on the merry-go-round of love twice more and fell off quickly. I remained open to possibility. I lost friends, family, and history. I gained better friends, a more honest family, and created a legacy. I travelled alone. I ate meals alone. I fell in love with myself.

In *Kramer vs. Kramer*, the husband and wife are in their early thirties. I am in my late forties. Meryl needed less filler than I do.

I am not concerned with the ideas of MARRIAGE and PERFECTION anymore. My son's custody schedule has been honored. I am resolute in dying HAPPY and being cremated. Cemetery plots are for maggots. It is my wish for my ashes to be spread through the most pristine pink waters in Harbour Island, Bahamas. This is by far, my favorite place on this earth. I am resolute in flipping a switch on how my movie ends. For three decades, I told myself a story of what life was supposed to be like. I rewrote that story. I am sharing it with you because this way, I ensure that you, the reader, will hold me accountable. We can change in one day.

Secret: This is not a rehearsal.

CHAPTER 10

i am not a victim.

Here is a story about a lovely lady (me) who was bringing up two very lovely boys.

It is really the story of me, my son, my stepson, and one life-changing Friday evening.

Mitch Albom is my favorite author. He has a quote, which I have on my refrigerator: "One day can bend your life." I was playing Legos with my son at 5 p.m. one Friday. My three-year-old son and I always practiced playing games that built, games that created strong foundations, games that taught. It was our way of having fun. I will never forget this day because it did bend my life in every way.

I am also a big believer in not chasing people or things, instead letting them land in your lap. Inevitably, the truth *always* lands in your lap. Anything you chase will escape you forever. I love truth, and the truth fell in my lap on this Friday evening. Literally, it slapped me in the face. I knew it was going to happen. Like the sun and the moon, the truth always comes out.

I was nineteen years old when I met my husband. My beliefs never wavered. I enthusiastically accepted his marriage proposal when I was twenty-five years old. When I accepted his first wedding ring—I had two—I told him, "Together, we can do anything. We can build a great life." I told him, "Before I say yes, the only thing I ask is that you never cheat on me."

He was cheating the day he proposed. Her name was Maribelle. She worked for him. They all worked for him. She knew me and my stepson. She was a poor soul that believed him, too.

Lies are the only thing I can't live with—infidelity. I just can't. It is the only thing I knew I could not forgive. I was a baby when I told him that, and I was resolute in this belief. I guess he thought I was kidding. I was tired of betrayal by the young age of seventeen.

Fast-forward to the year 2003, I had been with my family for seventeen years, and on this Friday, my story changed dramatically. The sun and the moon came out to grace me with my biggest fear. I ran to the door because I heard somebody knocking.

I lived in a historic home. The historic home needed an enormous amount of work, it was a 100-year-old home in the city of Coral Gables, Florida. The City Beautiful is what they call it. This home had its original cast iron bathrooms and tiny kitchen from a century ago. It was dated. This home was supposed to be my entire lifetime sanctuary. We hired a crew of approximately ten men to renovate it. The crew was led by an extraordinarily physically strong man, one who resembled Tarzan. He spoke terrible Cuban slang, a dialect. I knew he would get the job done. He was the manager of the renovation company. He was from the new Cuba. My ex-husband and I were from the first exodus. He was very fit. He was very loud. He was very friendly.

On this Friday in question, though, there was no work to do. I was a little perplexed as to why this man was knocking on my door. I opened the door with a bit of hesitancy—it was not a "Hey, how are you?" kind of greeting, it was more of an "Is there something wrong?" kind of greeting. I was very confused. I knew I had paid all the workers; I knew it was Friday, and my husband was out of town. He went out of town a lot. NUDGE, NUDGE, WINK, WINK.

As I held the door ajar, I asked, "What can I do for you?" He replied, "Well, I don't know." It was a very strange conversation. I continued with, "I already paid you, the tools have been cleaned up—did you leave something in the garage?" And he said, "Well, actually, I came to speak with you." At that moment, I knew my life was over. The life I knew, the strong foundation I had built, was about to fall apart.

I felt it.

My gut told me something excessively big was about to happen. I was right. Trust the gut.

I thought I was going to get raped and killed. He knew I was alone; he knew my husband was out of town. He knew my three-year-old could not run to the phone and dial 911. He was physically stronger than I was. And he knew the layout of the house very well. He even had the alarm code.

I was a sitting duck. A deer lost in the woods. I was scared.

Quickly, my mind travelled to protecting my son. How do I get someone here before I die? I truly felt I was going to die. I was right. I thought the man was going to rape and kill me. I was right. I knew it was bad, I just did not know what it was or how he was going to do it. I said, "Okay, give me a moment, let me settle my son and I'll be right out."

I closed and locked the door, got my cell phone and texted my cousin. My cousin and I grew up like sisters. She was the only other human being in the city that had the key. I wrote, "Please come here now, I'm in big trouble. I do not know what it is, but my son is in the house alone, hurry." When she confirmed she was on her way, I began unlocking the door. I threw my key into the bush so that this way, when he was done with me, he wouldn't be able to harm my son. With a bated breath, I walked outside.

I shakily asked, "What do you want to talk about?" He said, "Well, I'm here to tell you…. he does not love you. I love you, and you are going to die of AIDS if you stay with him."

He was trying to be elegant. I noticed he was using bigger words. He was trying to be professional. WTF was going on!? Who does not love me? Why are you speaking like this? I thought it was bizarre. Where was the meth? The bloopers camera crew? He continued, "I am trying to tell you that he doesn't love you and I do." I was still really confused. Before, I was just perplexed. I had a big question mark in my mind as to why he was here, and now, I was completely in the in the dark.

I felt like the little boy in *Different Strokes,* saying, "What you talking about, Willis?"

"He doesn't love you, but I do." I did not know who "he" was. I really was dumbfounded.

I was at a loss for words.

I had no idea what this man was saying. And then he said, "Your husband."

"Your husband doesn't love you."

My eyes swelled with tears and I fell on the floor. Boom, brother! I got it! I understand. I saw the light. I could not breathe. I could not speak. It felt like he did emotionally rape me. He did kill me. I died. My knees buckled. I was motionless.

I cried incessantly.

He said something that I knew, something that my heart had protected me from all those years. It felt like being hit in the head by Daniel La Russo's one-legged crane kick. All of a sudden, the Rolodex of the past almost twenty years flew through my mind. All the inconsistencies, all the open ends, all the loose ties came back and made sense now. They just flashed. My Rolodex flipped like a Studio 54 lit tsunami. The past twenty years of my life flashed through my mind like the worst hurricane ever, because I knew exactly what he was saying. My husband had been unfaithful.

Everything I wished for as a child was gone, everything I worked for as an adult was banished, and there was a handyman looking at me, professing his love as my three-year-old son waited for an SOS from my cousin. Why me? Why, GOD? Why me?

I knew it. I knew my life was going to change radically. I had no idea how bad this could hurt, and all I did was cry. I realized after about six solid minutes of crying—mucus running down my face, air escaping my body—that the man standing in front of me had a real crush. He was loving me hard as he tore my insides up. I also knew I was in physical jeopardy. I had to quickly gather my thoughts, understand where I was, and act. That is what you do, right? You assess your surroundings, and you adapt quickly, even if you have just been devastated. This was my superpower. I applied it. I looked up at him, and I said, "I love you, too."

A look of peace came over his face, and the sight of sheer pleasure was even more alarming. I had no choice but to say, "I love you, too." My life and the life of my son had been compromised. Our world had been breached. He was coming to save me from the big bad wolf, but at what price? I felt like I was on a tightrope. One wrong move and I would fall to my death. And if I fall to my death, what happens to the son I fought so hard to have?

Those six minutes seemed like an eternity, the most painful eternity I ever experienced. More painful than losing my father. I physically got up, my new "husband to be" or so he thought gave me a hand. I mean, it *is* the least he can do for the woman he loves, right? "Yes, indeed, I love you too," I repeated. "And we will be together."

I said that because I needed to buy time. How on earth could I love a man I barely knew? I needed to buy time to work through what he was saying. I knew in my heart there was truth to his claim—I just did not know how much overwhelming truth. I asked him how he knew. "How do you know this? How do you know that my husband does not love me?"

He said, very simply, "He told me."

Now you have to understand, after seventeen years of being with the same human being, after building a life, building a corporation, raising children, owning the stretch marks, going through the whole lifetime of commitment to hear a handyman, a glorified contractor (because he was an unlicensed contractor, in fact) say that my husband just simply *told* him was a Cobra Kai double kick to the soul. Bravo, bravo for simplicity.

I said, "I'm going to need a couple of days to investigate and absorb what you're saying, research and collect proof." He dutifully responded, "No, you don't need any proof, I've got all the proof." I said, "What do you mean you've got all the proof?"

My husband and I owned an office building together with his former partner. This building, which is now the Coral Gables Chamber of Commerce, is also in The City Beautiful. It is a beautiful place, and I encourage you to visit it if you are ever in the hood and want to network.

The handyman claimed that all the proof was in the office building. It made perfect sense that the demise of my marriage stemmed from the office: my former husband never liked it when I went there. I used to try to bring him lunch, I used to try to visit with our children, and he would push me away. I never understood why.

He kept telling me that I had no business being in the office. The office that I built, the office that I decorated, the office that I purchased, the office that I mortgaged myself for. He always told me I had no business being there, each time killing me more.

That Friday evening, I made it my business to go to the office—*my* fucking office. After I assured the handyman that we were going to live happily ever after, I sent him home. He was probably planning our wedding, but I was planning my defense. My cousin did arrive to take care of my son. I called a paralegal friend of mine to start the investigation, an attorney and a private investigator, and my mother, who lives in Canada. I had the team ready. I was hoping she could come because I knew that the weeks ahead were going to be exceedingly difficult. I made all the phone calls and set the wheels in motion.

I ate a pack of Marlboro Red cigarettes and dressed in black. I pulled my hair back in a ponytail and broke into my own real property. Ponytails are a bad sign. It was midnight and I was terrified. I went directly to where my new beau had sent me. I went for the corkboard, the Viagra, the cash, the phone book and the pictures. It was all there, exactly like he said. I had no idea my handyman ever even went to the office building.

In the City of Coral Gables, you pay high taxes. They protect their citizens well. If a burglar alarm rings in Coral Gables, the policemen are there in minutes. Lucky for me, the Coral Gables Chamber of Commerce building is located one minute away from the police station.

I knew I had sixty seconds to get proof of what this handyman was alleging and get out. I tapped into my best *Gone in Sixty Seconds* Angelina Jolie mindset and was successful. WooHOO! One good thing happened this Friday evening: I did not get arrested. The arrest comes later.

The handyman had specifically told me where to go to find these items. It was exactly as he described. Why would my husband take a Cuban handyman to our office building to gloat about how he cheats on me and then show him the proof?

This handyman had no business knowing what my office building looked like, and less business knowing so much about my family. The corkboard was the real dagger to the heart. I had hung it in the office to encourage a better culture within the firm. It was intended to elevate the firm's families and employees, but my ex-husband used it to hang his "real trophies" on it. Yes, he said that. "His real trophies" is what it was used for. What he was referring to were his conquests. His conquests were pinned on the board.

They were all his employees. His "real trophies" were women I had bought gifts for, had over for dinner, and treated as family for close to two decades. I am surprised he did not get sued for sexual harassment because 90% of the pictures on that board were employees. The employees of the firm were sleeping with the owners of this firm throughout its history. I had not only been fucked over by my husband but also by women I was kind to—many women. I ripped the pictures off the board and one by one went back in time together with professionals to begin learning the maze and wicked web of lies surrounding me. I stole the Viagra and gave it away (it was the Super-Size bottle). I never had sexual issues with my husband—or so I'd thought. I took the cash and spent it on Roman and my stepson.

I found all the information I needed to at least corroborate my death. It took me years to discover more women, and I still do not know if I know about all of them. And at this point, it is irrelevant. I asked him to never cheat. One or one hundred and one was just not relevant anymore. The police did come but I had already left the building. My fingerprints in that office were okay after all, I owned the building. It was the longest night of my life.

The handyman had told me the truth and nothing but the truth, and he did indeed save my life. He fell in love with me. He claims to have fallen in love with me because I used to feed all the workers at noon daily. I would plan family-style lunches for everyone. He saw me rear the children and work side by side with the crew. He felt sorry for me. I really hate it when people feel sorry for me. I am a big feeder. I love to feed. Please don't ever feel sorry for me.

My husband came home three days later. He was in Cuba. He claimed he needed to conduct business there. Last time I checked, Cuba was broke. The times he called to check on his son, I did not tell him I knew. My heart burned every time I heard his voice. I just gathered the information and blocked all feelings. I did not sleep. I did not eat. I worked. I put my head down and I worked.

When he came home, I made him his favorite meal. I served it to him like a dutiful wife. I was always a very dutiful wife. My father used to say, "Dutiful is beautiful." As he began to eat, I asked him one question. As I spoke, he acted as if he was disinterested in my question. I am sure he was. He was probably still reminiscing about the women in Cuba. He said, "Oh my God, what is it now?" as he rolled his eyes dismissively. I smiled like the Cheshire cat from *Alice in Wonderland* and asked him, "Have you ever been unfaithful to me?" He rolled his eyes again. He glared at me and said, "You are pathetic, desperate, and grasping at straws."

I handed him the dossier of information that the paralegal, private investigator, and I had collected over the weekend, combined with the stuff I had stolen from our office that confirmed he had cheated on me. I walked fearlessly to my bedroom and finally laid down to get some sleep. About thirty minutes later, he came upstairs and began to cry and professed his love for me. He told me how sorry he was, and that he would never do it again. The morning after, he cleaned out all the bank accounts.

I will never forget that handyman. He did indeed save my life.

A seven-year odyssey began.

I was raised by a wonderful father, and my father taught me to stand by my man through everything. I did do that. I honored my father's wishes through everything, through my ex-husband's ex-wife, through his ex-partner, through all the lies, through all the loose ends and the endless things that did not make sense. I used to get anonymous letters in the mail with pennies taped on them. I used to get threats, prank phone calls. I did not understand what was happening. I had trouble getting pregnant. I got an STD. He told me I got an STD because I sat on a toilet at a fair. The STD prohibited me from getting pregnant. It took me years to have my son. I do not know if it was solely the STD that delayed my pregnancy and I certainly did not sit on a public toilet at a fair. I am a fucking hypochondriac! I went through so much to find that everything I feared was true. The handyman solved my mystery. It was like a bad episode of *Forensic Files*. Mystery solved. No scientific DNA needed.

But what happened to the truth teller, my future husband? The handyman became an issue. He became a real problem for me. It was at the end of the renovation that it all came to fruition. I needed to get through that. I needed to finish our home. There was a lot of money on the line. I continued the farce of being in love with the handyman while I was finding information on what had happened in my adult life during my marriage, all at the same time. I lost thirty-two pounds in thirty days. I suffered adrenal gland failure. I ate incessantly, but it just ran through me like a river. I could not hold anything down. My life was over, and I was in my late thirties, and I was unemployed. Of course, I was the owner of the firm through marriage, but I had no real work experience from the past decade. I had turned down many great opportunities. I had a perfect offer for a job on the radio, and my husband had said, "No wife of mine will be on air." He was afraid I would find out. I had been lovingly raising my stepson and my son, building homes for us and supporting the corporation together with him. I wonder what my life what would have been like had I accepted that radio career.

You wake up and your life and everything you knew is gone. I am always, always going to be grateful to that handyman. I am also always grateful for any man that cheats on his wife and tells everybody in his city, including the handyman who spends endless days with his wife. He had such little regard for me and his family that he thought everyone in the world would agree with him on the definition of a "real trophy."

Secret: You don't have secrets, they have you.

CHAPTER 11

i am imperfect.

Of all the precious stones, pearls are my least favorite.

I like diamonds. To be specific, I love black diamonds. I think the mix of black and white diamonds is the most elegant. Black and white is worth the fight.

Pearls are not suitable for me. They are more appropriate for queens, princesses, and Nobel Prize winner types of women. I am not that type of woman. I tried to be that for my ex-husband, but it wasn't a good fit. I tried to be every woman for my ex-husband and it still wasn't a good fit. I am more of the rebel, thug type, the hardcore kind of jewelry wearer. I like chunks. Think LADY GAGA! Some folks may think my choice in jewelry is not ladylike, but who cares! My contract with H&H Jewels in Coconut Grove, Florida speaks for itself. If I am ladylike enough to represent a top jeweler, it is good enough for me.

The handyman (the lifesaver, the man in shining armor) insisted on giving me pearls. A big pearl, to be exact. WTF?

At the time of his jewelry offering, he was under the impression he was going to live happily ever after with me. He had indeed saved my life, right? He had just divulged privileged information that no one in seventeen years, including my family, ever did (my family knew, everyone knew). He had gone where no man had gone before. He told me the ugly truth. He had already given me the biggest gift I had ever received. He gave me freedom. A chance to live unencumbered of evil lies, betrayal, and fraud. This truth hurt like a motherfucker. I still was grateful. Even though it broke me in half, I was thankful.

Why was he so hellbent on giving me a fucking pearl, though? The truth hurt. It hurt like no pain I had ever experienced. And then, suddenly, he became obsessed with giving me a pearl.

You would think that someone else that knew I was being fooled would have told me beforehand. Perhaps my blood relatives, my neighbors, my friends, they could've dropped a hint, NOPE, it was THE HANDYMAN.

I love truth. It will always be the best gift you can give this girl.

Because he thought we were going to be together for the rest of our lives, he earned the privilege of giving me any jewelry he wanted. This was not a man of means; he was a construction worker. I tried to stop him from spending money on me as I knew there was no future. I told him to save his money and that I was not interested in monetary gifts. Finally, I hate pearls!

He kept insisting on giving me a pearl anyway.

I was losing my life to infidelity, scrambling to make sense of it all, shedding pounds by the minute, and now I was having to deal with a gift-returning issue. God laughs at people that make plans, doesn't he?

I pushed the pearl gift away for as long as I possibly could. I was still living under the guise of "I love you and we're going to ride off into the sunset together" in order to gather more information on my real life, my marriage, and its unraveling. That is a lot of pressure all at once. I could not keep lying to this man (the handyman, my truth teller): he was in my house every single day. We had been working together daily for months on bettering the historic property my family had purchased. It was a full court press about riding off into the sunset with me and living happily ever after since the day his truth rearranged my life. Think Lebron James coming at you. How does my cheating husband's way turn into me having to lie to a handyman daily? Gotta love a full court press!

I had to acquiesce and verbally accept the pearl, the jewelry, the gift. I had to buy more time. I reluctantly said, "Okay, you can give me the pearl. Thank you." It is not necessary, but he insisted. At this point, I would have said whatever he wanted to hear just to finish the renovations in the house and get more proof of what had happened to my life. I said, "Okay, whenever you want. Give me the pearl."

One fine day, we were finishing up the punch-out list for the historic home. I was relieved because I was going to get him—my knight in shining armor—out of my life once and for all. I was going to focus on either saving my marriage or walking away from it. Honestly, I knew at this point, I was just going to walk away from it. I was not trying to leave my entire years of adulthood, or the family that I desperately wanted as a child, but I knew I couldn't stay.

Betrayal of any sort is something I cannot live with. I have wicked trust issues.

I thought to myself, *I am finishing the real property improvements, getting rid of my admirer, and can now deal with my new reality in peace.* But wait, the pearl?

I had finally accepted the pearl verbally, but he never physically gave it to me. Phew, had I gotten away with it? Did he forget the whole pearl obsession? Had I escaped this?

The house was empty. Everyone had gone their separate ways. My son was at school, and there was no one in the home. The truth-giver was downstairs, and I was upstairs. I heard the footsteps of this new forever love of mine coming up, and I knew this would be one of our last moments together. He asked if he could give me the pearl. Really? Can someone just shoot me already? The last thing I wanted to do was accept a gift from a man, but I said, "Oh my God, please just give me the fucking pearl." I stuck out my hand and prayed he would just go away. He turned his back to me and began rifling through his jeans. I felt sorry for him. He was the only human who had the courage to tell me the unthinkable truth, and here I was: abusing him and taking his money in the form of an unwanted pearl.

I felt a brick, a thump land in my hand. This was no velvet box. No satin gift wrap. This was skin on skin.

I looked down to see the biggest penis I had ever seen in person sitting in my hand. It was the holder, the backdrop, the home of the PEARL.

I was going to smile and say thank you. Instead, I gasped and let his dick fall.

Hang on a second, are you telling me that the whole pearl inquisition was about his expectations of having sex with me?

Yep. His final gift on the way out of the house renovation was his dick, which had a huge pearl surgically inserted in the middle of the shaft. It was my going away prize.

I learned on that day that in Cuba, instead of getting tattoos and piercings, men would insert pearls or diamonds in their penis, to give the women that they had sex with more pleasure. This was the new version of Cuba, after my parents fled. I had never heard of this.

Am I lucky or what?

I want you to sit down for a minute and reread the last sentence. The pearl was in his penis. *There was a pearl in his penis.* I have seen a lot of tattoos and a lot of piercings in my lifetime, and I have met a lot of artsy people. I had NEVER dreamed of seeing anything like this, never mind accepting it as a going away gift.

Once again, I was scared for my life. Twice in a month, I had been attacked with truth that even a sci-fi thriller could not recreate. I cannot lie, though: this shock was more pleasant than the last one.

I smiled at him. We had sex for hours.

I gave him a going away gift. We engaged in raw, passionate, sex. He was extraordinarily strong in every way. This was not the best decision in my life, I promise. But I do not regret it. He took a huge risk in telling me the truth about my life. I was grateful.

What bothered me about this was I knew there was no future with him, and he believed there was. He was in love with me, and I was not in love with him. I highly recommend having sex with a man that has a pearl in his penis, however. It's liberating.

I had sex with him nonstop for weeks. When the construction was over, and the renovation came to an end. We paid him what we owed him. Then, I mustered up the resilience and said, "Listen, this is just not going to work. I must go through a lot of legal issues. I do not know if I am going to get a divorce. And I really do not want to ride off into the sunset with you."

Welcome to the Twilight Zone again! My biggest fan turned into my biggest stalker. He began to follow me around. He prank-called me fifty times a day for weeks. He threatened me and my family. It became a nightmare. I knew I would be writing a book back then. You just can't make this shit up. It was a mess. A complete mess.

I ended up getting a restraining order against my savior, my truth teller, my handyman. He did eventually go away.

There are reasons why people come into your life. He came into mine to save me and to introduce me to pearls.

I still do not wear pearls. I laugh every time I see one.

Secret: If you're going to ever give me a gift, know that the truth is what I need more than anything else and black diamonds are my favorite.

CHAPTER 12

i am a convicted felon.

When you think about a thug life, you think about a chopper in the car and forensic science. You think about those television shows with the creepy man voice narrating, shows like *Cops* and *24 Hours*. You do not think about a married couple in Coral Gables having a domestic violence brawl in front of their million-dollar historic home. But this is *my* thug life, not a TV show, my real life. And in my life, anything is possible.

I went to jail for the second time because I had a fist fight with my ex-husband. The first time I went in, I was charged with racketeering and mortgage fraud. This must be one of the weirdest stories I have ever witnessed. Never mind, been a part of. #KEEPITWEIRD. I was the leading lady in this show. I was the protagonist. It is still unbelievable to me. I think about going to jail often. It keeps me humble. #FuckDaPolice. I cannot believe that was me, but indeed, it was. And that is me on the cover of this book: no face beat, no filters, no lighting. Just me, a convicted felon. When somebody threatens your children, the real public enemy is born.

My son was threatened on this day. His religion was threatened. His freedom to choose was threatened. The Incredible Hulk became real. I closed the domestic violence episode in front of the Spanish-style historic home with a razor-sharp *Jaws* bite to my ex-husband's left shoulder. I am not proud of this. However, fucking with a child in front of me is a bad idea, especially my own. I am a physically abused child. I was a child that was abused. I do not take kindly to child abuse of any sort. It is a cowardly act to harm someone that is lesser. The drive to protect your child becomes venomous adrenaline. It is unmatched strength.

I had never in my life felt so much rage. I had taken various self-defense classes in my life, and I proudly applied what I'd learned in all of them. I ask myself if I would do this again. And the answer is yes. I would protect any child from any harm against anyone forever. What I learned in jail was extensive; please grab a notepad and start taking notes. This is your survival guide, in case you ever end up in the can. A crime of passion CAN happen to anyone. One day can bend your life. I was in and out of three local Florida jails in thirty-two hours. I was driven in three government vehicles. I was chained to other inmates. It was freezing. It was always freezing.

They gave me an orange uniform. Orange is my least favorite color.

Shop Splash did not sponsor this photo shoot. No bra was provided, but they did give us Underoos (grandma panties with no elastic). I guess they were afraid I would Epstein myself. I was given green foam slippers with a happy face on them. Bet you did not know green was the happiest color on the wheel. I was not strip-searched. Can I get an AMEN?

I met so many abused women. I made friends in jail. I am just like them. I am just like you. I taught a yoga class. It was quite different from the classes I teach today at Sol Yoga in Wynwood. It was vastly different from the classes I take at Anatomy at 1220. The foods served were not foods at all. The bread had mold on it and the Spaghetti-Os consisted of a bowl of red liquid with three circles floating on the top.

Allergies are not an option in jail. I did not eat anything. I did not drink water. No one cared. I peed once. I did not bathe. I was very cold. The purpose of making it so cold, was to prevent outbreaks. The tempers and noise levels in jail are high, remarkably high. It was apparent that, at any moment, a fist could come flying across the room. My crime was a crime of passion. So were theirs. We are the same.

The female inmates were beautiful. They were beautiful on the outside and emotionally destroyed on the inside. We were all broken. Jail is no bueno. Spirituality was nonexistent. The stories had different names but were not so different at all. We were paraded by male inmate cells and corridors. The men were aiming and shooting their semen at us trying to make contact with any woman they could. It missed me by a smidgen. I almost vomited. It was not sexy. There were enormous cockroaches everywhere; I had never seen such bugs. At least there were no lizards. The toilet was aluminum. It was a hole in the ground. Yes, you had to pee in front of everyone. Was it humiliating? Of course. At one point, I asked a guard for a piece of fruit, as a healthy option, and her response was, "This isn't a hotel."

In the United States, we have more humans in jail than any other place in the world. This is blasphemy. The reason I taught the yoga class was because the girls became agitated. I spoke truly little in the cells. I predominantly listened. I knew I would be getting out quicker than they would. I grew through the trauma. I listened as the conversation amongst my new room-mates and new posse became increasingly heated. I was afraid I was going to have to defend myself physically yet again. I have been defending myself physically all my life. I used some of my prana wisdom and took a great risk to control situations.

I was afraid they would notice I was different. I was afraid they would notice I was well-spoken. I was afraid they would notice I was from another tax bracket. I toned down all the fancy and tapped into my newly-discovered street credz. Call me LIL REV, LIL MAG—just please do not call me an on-the-board, contributing community member and Coral Gables resident. During yoga classes, instead of referring to the ujjayi breath, I said, "Let us breathe like the ocean sounds." I broke through to them. I connected to my #ganggang. We began to flow in baby steps as one. We were united. In the end, we were all one.

We are all united. It worked like magic. They began to share, divulge the reasons they were in the cell with me. I was horrified. Why, why, why? The common thread was crimes of passion. It was love, lack of love, not enough love, misunderstood love, peculiar love. I learned a new word. I learned what ZOOTED meant—it means getting high. When it was time to speak of tax returns in front of one another, I froze. There is no privacy in jail. You cannot whisper. There is no freedom in jail: you cannot hide. When a guard asks you how much money you report on your tax return, you answer. Even if you are locked in a room with humans that cannot afford to eat. What are the United States thinking?

This system makes more felons, more convicts, and more victims, but I did make genuine connections in that jail. When I was released, I went to visit my friend. I went to her church. I taught the children of the church how to share. I spent a day with the mothers, teaching them how to exercise. I asked my brands to donate merchandise and money. They did, and I delivered it. I am no stranger to the homeless. I have been serving the less fortunate all my life.

When I left the jail and was released, I went home. I was beat, mentally exhausted. I was Offset and Cardi B, all in one. I was Charles Manson reformed and the Messiah found. I bathed in hot water in privacy for a long time. My skin shriveled up like a prune. I needed to cleanse. I ate nutritious foods. A *lot* of healthy foods. I needed to nourish. I was ready to bounce back again. I went to my computer and there she was. I met the Communist Terrorist for the first time.

She would make my life unbearable for the next seven and a half years. She is the attorney who was hired by my ex-husband to finish me off. It always makes me laugh when you meet a woman that works against other women. COMMIES!!

This is her job. It is not her fault entirely. It is her job, and I could not do her job. But there is nothing like being a woman that supports other women. I would not be able to sleep at night knowing I was harming another woman.

The judge in my case was also a woman. This, too, is public information. I want you to research the names in my case, I want you to learn who the players were.

It was an omnibus of abuse, I was slaughtered like a marielita coming from Cuba on a tire. It didn't matter to me, really. My son was protected and no one was lying to me.

Divorce in the State of Florida is bullshit.

My son witnessed what happened in my domestic violence case. It was one of the saddest days of my life. I have included the mugshot for your perusal. I chose it intentionally. It does not even look like me. I felt it poignant to share this photograph. I am proud of myself for defending my son and his religious rights. His autonomy to choose is his constitutional and GOD-given right. I am proud of my will to stop the abuse towards me and my son. I had been emotionally, sexually, mentally, and physically abused all my life. I am proud of all the strength training that I mastered. The cover of this book memorializes it all.

I hope that my sharing this very painful moment in my life helps you to understand that a crime of passion can happen to anyone at any time. Yes, it can happen to you. What would you do to protect your child? What wouldn't you do?

I want to help expose this tragedy because it is mine. It is my divine right to do with this tragedy whatever I want. I hope it helps someone, anyone. I am not worried about what people think of me or what I looked like on the day I went to jail. It is kind of hard to keep it sexy under these circumstances. I mean, let's be honest, I am the highly photogenic @revete. I am more worried that there are people going through these tragedies, thinking that they are alone. They are not alone. You are not alone. We are all the same. We are all united. I was afraid of telling this story for a few years; the Communist Terrorist is always ready to fire. I thought about how I would be perceived and criticized, and then I thought about the men that assault women every minute of every day and think that they can continue as if nothing happened. I thought about the children that are abused every minute of every day and cannot help themselves.

I thought about my son.

He was exhausted of being indoctrinated to a religion that was foreign to him. I have never hit my son or any other person without provocation in my life. I do not believe in physical violence. We are not animals; we are not savages. If you need to say something, you use your words. I have been raised and surrounded by people that claim to love me and murdered me time and time again, both emotionally and physically.

I never agreed with it. I never agreed to it. I got tired of it. The day that I had that domestic violence episode with my ex-husband solidified my feelings towards all forms of abuse, once and for all. I think the next time someone raises a hand to me, they'll think twice.

The experience of going to jail was like watching the longest Jerry Springer episode ever created. I love Jerry Springer—he is my hero and now a judge.

When we watch television shows in regard to jail we assume that some of it or a lot of it is drama.

I assure you, there is truly little drama involved. It is exactly what happens. In my case, I was taken to the Coral Gables police station first. It was the Ritz-Carlton compared to what I was about to face. Ironically, it was one block away from the place that stored all the wrongdoing towards me and my marriage: my ex-husband's office.

I was convicted of the crime of domestic violence. This, too, is public information: the state of Florida versus Magda Lopez was born.

I want you to focus on the names of the attorneys that sacrificed my life, my money, and my future. I know you are going to Google this. I want you to learn the name of the only attorney that restored my faith in the law, the attorney with a good heart. He saved me from the Communist Terrorist. His name is Steven Nullman, and he was the founder of Nullman Law. I am going to shout that name loud and proud for the rest of my life. He is the best family lawyer in Miami, Florida.

When I arrived at the Coral Gables police station, the officers misled me and told me I would be leaving in two hours. This was a blatant lie, the first of many lies that I would hear for the next thirty-two hours. Approximately five hours later, I was chauffeured to another jail. Here, I was informed that I would not be leaving jail until I calmed down. I was calm. I just got assaulted and arrested, but it is in my nature to remain calm when under pressure.

I was happy. I was assaulted. I fought back. I would do it again. The trip to the jail was my first experience in a government van with no windows. I have Scoliosis, and I was bent over like the Hunchback from Notre Dame.

I was chain-linked to other human beings.

This was the first time that has ever happened to me.

Luckily, there was no smell in this Uber.

I was processed at the second jail and given an orange inmate uniform, extralarge Underoos, and the happy face green slippers again, which I still have. #shoegamestrong. The reason they give you the foam sandals in the color green is so you don't beat anyone else. You stay happy, Pharrell would disagree with this. Pharrell sings the song "HAPPY". Does green indeed make people happy? Really? The State of Florida thinks so. I do not agree.

It is freezing in jail. It's so cold that you get a cold.

The reason it is this way is to isolate human beings. It is inhumane. Most of the women in the female prison were exactly what we see on television, exactly what we see on Jerry Springer. My new family, these women, my new peer group, my gang were all in for the same crime. Some of these women were gorgeous. The lack of education in jail is startling; most of the women never graduated from high school.

They were torn, and exhausted. I was too. A lot of them were mothers. A lot of them were drug users. In the process of my knowing these ladies, I made friends.

We connected.

I was very scared.

I was transferred to the third jail. Eighteen hours later.

Once again, I was chain-linked, bent over like a hunchback put in a dark van with no windows. And this time, there was a stench. It smelled. No one bathes in jail. They get wet, but soap is foreign.

I had little interaction with the showers. I did not use them. I think about me going to jail and COVID-19, and I thank God that wasn't happening at this time.

Making a phone call in jail is virtually impossible. You don't have Google, you don't have a phonebook, you don't have time. There was a line of people three blocks long desperately seeking release. It is pandemonium.

I felt helpless. I tried to remember survival in Lord of the Flies.

There was a fight in the third jail—I ignored it. It had to do with somebody's braids. Braids are all the rage in prison.

I had free time in jail; I did not use it. I just stared in silence, assessing what had happened to me. I taught the girls breathing exercises in order to lower their heart rate and calm their minds. I taught them how to pray in Sanskrit. Everybody found their center.

I escaped what could have turned into a violent war in a tiny little cell. Instead, I turned it into a variation of meditation.

I noticed that there was no security to help us in case a fight arose. In jail, no one cares about human life.

There was blood and feces all over the cells. Where do our tax dollars go?

No wonder my body stopped functioning. I was shy. I did not get the cavity search that many people ask me about. I talked my way out of it. I had some leftover cream on my body, body cream from Victoria's Secret that had sparkles and glitter. I was almost assaulted twice because of the glittery cream. It shines like jewelry; people thought it was valuable. They wanted to take it off my body.

Despite the Instagram posts, I am a very private person. I have big boobs—my boobs weigh me down. The fact that they did not give me a bra was killing my back and not assisting the Scoliosis. They gave me one thin bed sheet to spend the night. The mattress imitation was made of vinyl. It was thinner than the worst toilet paper I had ever touched. You freeze at night.

You just freeze.

The woman in my cell with me cried all night. I tried to calm her down, but she did not speak.

Jail is worse than what we see on TV. Much worse.

The guards look like sergeants from Iraq. They do not smile. They do not make eye contact. You are a nonfactor. *I* was a nonfactor.

I connected with some of the friends I made in jail on social media—they are as important to me as the highest paid professional on my friends list. Life is about learning from human beings, growing from human beings, elevating human beings. My time in jail was not in vain. It memorialized my relationship with my ex-husband and memorialized my relationship with my mother. I was tired of being abused.

In my life, I suffered an enormous amount of abuse. That strike to the face was the end. It was my breaking point. He was trying to take my phone out of my hand, but the fist hit the cheek and the GAME was ON!

Post Malone says that going to jail is like taking a break. I understand what he means. It is a different society. It is a different community. You do not pay taxes, you do not have to worry about being cheated on, you do not have to worry about making appointments.

It is the worst thing in the world, losing your freedom. I will never forget it. It keeps me humble.

When I think about the fight the fight itself, it wasn't the strike to the face that did it. It wasn't the provocation of my son's religious beliefs being compromised alone. It was a lifetime of injustice.

Jail taught me humility, gratitude, and lessons you cannot get until you hear the slam of the door to your own jail cell. It taught me that the law does not protect you. It taught me that crooked lawyers and judges exist. It taught me that family connections in the legal system work. Just because someone hits you and you defend yourself does not mean you're correct. It just means you are me, them, and possibly you.

I am a LEO. I would kill to protect my son or any other child. If it happens again, I'd do it again. I'm not righteous. I'm not claiming to be right. It is my inherent belief that when you have a child, you protect them at all cost. My father did this. I did this. I hope my son does this.

When something threatens your child in any way, you defend at all costs.

People laugh all the time and ask me about the infamous bite, and about my time in jail. I have never been so candid about my time in jail as I have now, in this book. I hope it is a constant reminder that injustice can be just and therapeutic.

This is my tattoo. This is my book. This is my photograph. This is my conviction. I hope that you show this photograph to anyone that has ever been abused. I hope you share my story with anyone that needs it. I hope that they find the strength that I found.

I hope they are not afraid of judgment. I hope they walk firmly and fearlessly in their journey.

I am proud of my jail journey: it made me who I am.

This chapter is to expose a photograph.

This chapter is to expose vulnerability.

I want to take the privilege away from anyone that circulates this picture and give it back to its rightful owner- me! Feeling shame is not something I am guilty of.

Everything I do—including going to jail—I do to the best of my ability.

I want to expose that it is possible to turn a wrong into right.

I am a convicted felon. Next?

Secret: Who are you?

CHAPTER 13

i am @revete.

My son walked up to me while I was in the kitchen one day and said, "Hey Mom, you should get on Instagram." I remember saying, "Honey, I don't play those games." He said, "No, Mom, this is the future, it's not Pokémon. Everyone is on Instagram. It's like a big photo album." I should have known then that my @REVETE life was about to explode on little squares all over the world.

Social media was revolutionary in my life. Social media became a noticeably big truth in my daily habits.

I started the @REVETE page on that day. I was skeptical: remember, I am highly paranoid. I have O.C.D. and thick walls all around me. I was new to this, but how hard could it be? I won Social Head in Bethany year after year by landslides. Popular is something that comes naturally to me. I did not see the point, really, but anything Roman suggests, I seriously contemplate.

I certainly did not see the financial potential, either. I never imagined I would be earning income on social media. I am very private. It was absurd to me that posting your life could make you money. I know you are laughing right now. *If she's so private, why did she write a book?* But I gave up on the notion that there is anything private left after social media became my brave new world. Nothing is private. Do not fool yourself. Everything is public. In a way, I like it because fuckers cannot hide anymore. CHEATERS, beware.

On the flip side, I hate it because I cannot seek shelter anymore. I often wonder how J. Lo handles life. Whether you have social media, whether you use social media, it does not matter. There is a jackass somewhere that is going to post evidence of you at a party with someone you were not supposed to be with anyway. Govern yourself accordingly. You cannot control the rest of the world. Whether you are on social media or you have been put on social media unbeknownst to you, it just does not matter: you are exposed. We are all the same. When I came to this factual realization, I decided to explore monetizing it. I never fight with seizure of opportunity. I am the daughter of Cuban immigrants. Dale!!!!

It worked like magic. I have no secrets; I live secret-free. Therefore, my fear of invasion of privacy has disappeared. Poof, be gone! I am the same on and off social media. I curse regularly. I eat unhealthily now and again. I always have the same people with me. And I am not afraid of exposing it. I know myself, therefore, I am myself. It is easy. I get criticized for this carefree view daily. I am not for everyone, and that is okay by me.

On Instagram, I can elevate brands, clients, and healthy causes. I thrive in this make-believe community. In one post, I can reach millions of humans—that's genius. My social media is NOT a big photo album like my son explained approximately eight years ago. It is a tool I use to earn income. I do not rant about my personal feelings ever on this format. I do not seek revenge on any humans that hurt me in the past. It is work, and it is money-producing.

Many companies began to ask me how I use my media. What methodology was I applying? I was hired countless times to run other accounts. Currently, I am under contract with some of Miami's finest companies. I had to learn the language of cost per post, per engagement, insight development, and how to charge for all of this. I read, I learned, I grew. Just add this language to the other five I speak. I believe my age has a lot to do with my success in this AI world. Young influencers only care about how they look, but I really could give a flying fuck about that. I care about selling the product. I care about closing the deal. I care about getting the job done. It is an age thing.

Being passionate is in me. Being social is in me. Social media wins with people like me.

There is no room for shy in a shameless selfie.

The first time I was hired to model, I was eleven years old. The commercial was for Coca-Cola. I was on film before Instagram was born. I stayed short, so a future in modelling died quickly. I still did ad work for face and upper body whenever I could. It was easy and, once again, shy I am not!

About eight years ago, I learned that my photographs combined with my method of engagement became art. Smart art! I began working with fitness companies, nutrition companies, doctors, dentists, lawyers, automobile corporations, etc. I would get whatever I wanted for trade and get paid just for showing up. I am not a celebrity or a model or an influencer. I am a woman that causes an effect. I always have been. I always will be. I have NEVER endorsed or supported any product, cause, or brand I did not love. Thankfully, I have been able to pick and choose agency at leisure.

Party execution is something I am good at. I love a good party! When local venues, professional teams and companies began requesting my presence, the real explosion occurred. I found myself almost kissing Lil Pump, dancing with athletes, and splashed all over media. More coverage, more hires. Magda became @REVETE. I #LOL hard when people call me that. BTW, I really don't like it when people LOL me. The word is ATREVETE. it means to dare. The slogan for my company is my mantra: "Dare to be different."

@REVETE is not my name. The girl people see on media looks nothing like me. I seldom wear makeup or fancy clothes in real life. You can always find me in a ponytail or bun and in workout gear. That is the real me. @REVETE is much more sophisticated. I prefer Magda over @REVETE, but I do what the payer wants. The client, the customer, the consumer is ALWAYS right. I wish all businesses applied this rule.

My powerful relationships are really what makes me the brand I am. I keep tight, loyal, and safe relationships in all aspects of life. I DO NOT CHEAT on my clients. I AM NOT A CHEATER! This attribute has brought me an enormous amount of business. I am eternally grateful for the alliances I have made in the past decade. Loyalty always wins.

I have learned that an almost fifty-year-old woman can sell anything better than a twenty-year-old woman with a good caption, hashtag, and location. Who gives a fuck about cellulite? Have you ever heard of FACETUNE?

I have also learned that, unless you are married and in a secure personal relationship, you should separate your romantic life from media. I made the mistake of exposing one of my baby loves and am still trying to disassociate myself from that former relationship. Catching a cheater is fun on media.

You can do it in five minutes flat. It is easy. Transparency is the best way to thrive on media and in life. Being genuine sells!!!

Social media can be an extremely dangerous place. You are vulnerable. I remember the first time I received a negative and hurtful comment. I cried. It hurt. I could not understand why someone would hide behind a fake account just to insult you. It did not make sense, but it still hurt. It never hurt again after that. My skin grew thick quickly. I send hearts to all hateful comments now. My presence and involvement on these platforms, channels, and self-broadcast is for one purpose only: MONEY!

Because I am almost fifty years old, I know life is delicious. I remember life before media. I have better things to do in this life. It is a job, people. It is not real. I regularly go to schools and teach why this is harmful to adults and children equally. It is just decoration, smoke and mirror.

I remember living life without media and still selling, closing, and invoking emotion just by walking into a room. I transferred that talent to my iPhone. Boom, @REVETE makes a statement.

If you've learned anything from this book, you already know this is easy for me. It is fun and supplemental income. It's like a side chick. If you get too involved in computers, insights, and information on platforms as a reality, you LOSE! If you get too involved with side chicks, YOU LOSE MOST!

If you notice, all my posts show an enormous amount of love and adoration. You rarely see the haters. There are more haters than there are lovers. It does not matter, though: approval of me is not the goal. Sales, retention, and awareness are the goals.

I have made so many great relationships on media, it's SICK! My highest grossing Fortune 500 Coaching engagement came through Instagram, too. You must be able to decipher the truth from lies quickly. I DO NOT ANSWER DMS! I post Monday through Friday, with few exceptions. I never exceed 1,000 posts, because I delete old commercials and ads with new ones. I use Twitter as a business platform, Facebook as a local conduit, and LinkedIn for my son. Instagram is my forte.

I would be remiss not to mention some of the companies that have supported @REVETE and Magda since day one. These companies are solid. They are true, and I highly recommend them on and off media. Thank you to Alex and Caro Pirez from Body and Soul Miami, Sylvia from Milan Pole Dancing Studio, Marc Megna and Chris Paciello from Anatomy at 1220, Cathy DeFransesco from Sol Yoga Miami, Liana of Miami Magazine, EVERYONE at CBS4, P at Mercedes-Benz of Coral Gables, Ivette (my stylist) and Bibi from Shop Splash, Andy (hottest dentist) Bliss Dental Miami, Jesse at Miami Heat, Nicole, Jake, Katerina at The Florida Panthers, Phil Shechter, CPA, Steven Nullman, ESQ, Phil at Soho Beach House, Ashley at Beauty By Nuvo, Ashwin at Nuvoyou Med Spa, Everyone at HH Jewels, Alejandro Chaban at Yes You Can, Grant Weeditz at Weediddy, Mimi at Mimilicious Mia, Toni at TaskHappy by Toni, Jesse at Hyde Arena, everyone at Grown, Mike at Lyfe Brand, D at The Vive Hydration, Rob Crosoli at E11even, Youseff at Delmonte, Nancy at Kobi Karp, Joe and Manning at Legacy Fit, Bobby and Lisa at Bobby Maximus, Lia Aimes and Rich Wilkerson at Vous Church for loving me. All of these humans helped my growth on media and personally. Deeply grateful.

The BLOCK feature is my favorite. I have thousands of accounts BLOCKED. I do not hesitate to push this button, on and off media. If a fucker is going to hate, what is there to think about? Audit, audit, audit.

One of my brands named this chapter for me. Originally, I was going to call it "Girls on Film." She renamed it "Everyone loves Magda." I laughed endlessly, then renamed it again. Everyone does not love Magda, because very few people know Magda. Brands and consumers alike benefit from Magda on media and if I agree, I benefit from them equally. It is an agreement—a contract, in fact. I do NOT wake up in the morning looking for new friends, approval, or love on media. I am looking for numbers, growth and education. If this is interpreted as love for me, I welcome it all. I am grateful for this method of earning. It is fun, fresh and ever changing. It is effective. If social media ever stopped, I would still be an effective salesperson, ambassador, representative. I am impervious to this. It is a challenge to remain sane through this lightning speed maneuvering of the world, but I love to DARE!

I follow very few people on media. This is not a ploy or a tactic. This is business. If I follow you, it is for money, not love. If I love you, you know it blindly. Real love can never be given or accepted on a computer platform. #NGL.

Secret: I love my privacy.

CHAPTER 14

i am a lover.

You are just my type. But what is my type? What is a type?

The first time I thought I was in love; I was thirteen years old and he was twenty-eight. My mother left me in his care. He taught me how to write checks to pay for bills. He showed me what I had to write on every line and why—I will always be grateful for this lesson. He taught me how to cook. He was Italian. The dishes were all in red sauce. He conditioned me to live in a way that led me to believe I was his and he was mine.

My mother had to travel a lot for work. I was alone in another country without adult supervision. Is that a type, an educated choice, or statutory rape? This was clearly rape. I thought he would be my husband. Isn't that the logical conclusion? In my teenage mind, I was lovingly being handed off to a man that loved me.

Unbeknownst to me and my mother, he was already married. His wife's name was Antonia. That is my middle name. The irony is funny. My mother needed a babysitter, and he took advantage of a defenseless child. He shattered my heart and erased my innocence forever. Trust took flight and never came back. He was my first betrayal. I do not know what it is about me that almost guarantees every time I make myself vulnerable to a man, he cheats! This time, I had no choice in this vulnerability.

This experience laid the groundwork for the same pattern in my adult personal relationships. Of the four relationships I've had that I consider real, only one man was faithful. What is faithful? My favorite response to this question is: "As long as I don't fuck someone else, I am faithful." If you lie, hide, hold an emotional connection with a third person, it is over. This includes phone games, omission, hidden texts, and all that jazz.

Because of this first experience with what I understood as love, following relationships were excruciatingly difficult for me. It takes so much out of me to make myself vulnerable. I feel like I am setting myself up for imminent death always. Notwithstanding, I keep getting on the merry-go-round. What is life without love? It took me almost fifty years to find out that love is not a man and a woman living together in marriage. Love is so much more. I know that now. I could not possibly grasp the concept at thirteen. We grow up at love looking through the lens of our parents: my father preached traditional marriage as successful love, and my mother left me alone. I had no choice but to seek the result that was instilled in me at an incredibly young age. I died five times trying to fulfill my father's idea of successful love.

I do not know if I have a sign on my forehead that says, "Yes, come fool me." Why is it even a thing, fooling people? How is that fun?

I was thirteen years old. I did not stand a chance. I am forty-nine now, and my rapist still calls me and tells me he loves me. Although it is nice to know that he thinks of me and holds me as a fond memory, his love did enormous damage in my life. He should have gone to jail. Someone should have been protecting me from him. He should have seen that he would forever impair me from knowing how to love and be loved properly. I never felt love for another man in Canada again. There was a point in my life where I felt I couldn't be loved.

My second love was a Miami man named Chris. (Notice how I feel comfortable mentioning his name.) The reason I feel safe saying his name is he DID NOT CHEAT! (Pinch me.) After the rapist, Chris was a breath of fresh air. The worst thing Chris did was get too high. In comparison to the rapist, this was fine by me. I have little issue with the use of marijuana. I do not like it or need it, but it doesn't bother me when others use it. I feel that alcohol is more an enemy.

Chris was an enigma to me. He perhaps was the best-looking man I ever dated. He was age appropriate; he was very faithful. I wanted to marry him. He was simple. He was strong. The issue here was drugs. For me, hard drug usage is a dead end. How could I have a family with someone drug dependent? My father was on air and I was living in Miami. How would this look?

I tried everything I could to help Chris. I reached, searched, and fought, but to no avail. I was thrust into a world that I luckily did not comprehend. I knew there was no future with this situation. I knew this would kill us. Because I had such a tumultuous childhood, the thing I needed most from a man was stability. Drug usage robs you of stability in every way. Marijuana was not the issue: it was the drugs I had never seen before, highs that were too scary to identify and a world I wanted no part of. I still think of him often and wish things would have been different. He had a heart of gold: I felt protected with him. He was my first orgasm—it was five years of being sexually active and it took a FAITHFUL man to bring me to orgasm. It was this quality about Chris that confirmed my connection between heart and body. Love is protection. I hate drugs.

The love that came after that was the most exciting. It was my husband. Husband is king. Husband is the highest after my father and son. I spent twenty stable years with my husband. There were no drugs involved. He was perfect, or so I thought. I did not care what he looked like. To me, he looked like a God. He gave me everything I wanted. He saved me. He restored my faith in men and family. With him, I did not have to protect myself from anyone—again, or so I thought. I could finally trust—or so I thought. I was protected—or so I thought. I was not getting raped—or so I thought.

He brought stability to a broken girl. He swore he would never be unfaithful. He was a GOD-like creature. I had finally achieved what my father wanted for me, and I was the opposite of what my mother showed me. I never wanted to be a single, independent career woman. I wanted to be a wife and a mother. I DID IT! It was kind of like a fairy tale ending for me. And then, it also turned out to be the worst drama horror movie ever. It was the most devastating betrayal of my life. I am surprised that I even lived through it. I really wanted to die. Notwithstanding, where the fuck is the merry-go-round?

I had two brief baby loves after my husband knocked my knees off and… drumroll please, they too thought the grass was greener on the other side. They stayed on that side. I left them there. They were kids trapped in men's bodies.

I spent three years with a younger man after my husband. It was fun. We travelled a lot. I paid a lot. Is this what a cougar is? I guess I was a cougar. I am still not sure if he absolutely loved me or was just absolutely using me financially. I feel like relationships are two people agreeing to better each other. I bettered him. He wasted my time. Age is not the issue for me and never was. I believe that two people that want to make a union work can. Fuck age. The only stipulation is to be invested entirely. All in or all out.

After this baby love, I robbed the cradle again with another younger man. This relationship was the weakest and the shortest, but I did honestly love him. His form of cheating was social media. Cheating takes place on social media often. Duh, you can see a cheater on media in two seconds. This relationship was the last straw. I became a smoker again. And I never wanted to see a fucking merry-go-round again.

Dating now is an entirely other book. No one is really single. Either they are in an imaginationship, a situationship, or living with toxicity. I can't be bothered by this shit. Either you are in it to win it or you are just playing. I have NEVER been interested in transient sexual and momentary relationships. I want the entire EVER AFTER. I always have. This could possibly land me a role in a *Bridget Jones' Diary* movie. I am okay with being alone. I am not okay with living a lie.

Dating is not for me. I have no time or interest for liars, bullshit, or wasting time.

Every time I meet a man and like him, I tell him upfront: "I have been fucked over hard, are you loyal?" I have yet to meet the man that says no! I would probably hug him tight. Honesty is so fucking attractive.

A type. It is still so confusing to me. If I sit and analyze the five men I have loved, which I do often, I cannot help but notice how incredibly different they were. Radically different. The only common thread I can identify is that each one of them had a superpower, a major attribute that set them apart from the majority. Each man stood out in a crowd. I prefer to swim in the minority, the elite, the few, the proud. Other than this similarity between the lucky five, there are no commonalities. I really don't have a type.

There is no common physical denominator, either. Their nationalities were so different—I am an equal opportunity lover, you know, multicultural. Their education levels were insanely different as well. A doctorate or a GED makes no difference to me. Loyalty is the degree I need to make any real relationship work.

What is my type?

After going up to bat five times wholeheartedly in half of a century, I have decided that the best love grand slam I could ever make is choosing myself. I am my type. I am protected. I am unusually strong. I work to be what I want in my relationship daily. However, I wish I could share that in good health with a committed significant other, #NGL. There is no doubt I long for marriage and family still. I am often asked why I still believe in love, fidelity, and the sanctity of marriage after all the betrayal. I passionately do. I always will. My commitment to those beliefs is unwavering. I am often questioned on why I am alone after close to a decade of divorce. I will NOT SETTLE again. ALL IN or ALL OUT with complete commitment. I am not thirteen anymore.

For a woman that excels, wins, and succeeds a lot, I have always lost in love. In this aspect, I cannot seem to win. Maybe winning here is always being at a loss. I will let you know in the next book. Maybe my next book will be on dating. Maybe it will be about successful and honest love with a man or on my own. NUDGE, NUDGE, WINK, WINK.

Anything is possible. I remain hopeful for safe, protected, and loyal love one day.

Secret: I DO know a man who currently has everything he needs to be my next king. He is my shooter. His name is Ron, I believe in him. (Notice how I am unafraid to say his name.) Cross your fingers.

CHAPTER 15

i am a cowboy.

My father's initials were E.P.D. His name was Enrique Pedro de la Torre. E.P.D. in Spanish also stands for "en paz descanse," which means rest in peace. I hope he is resting. I know he wouldn't be too happy with my ex-husband, but otherwise, he should be resting soundly. He lived large, left a legacy, and created a great story.

He was the ultimate smoker. He smoked two packs of Pall Mall cigarettes daily—the cigarettes with no filter. He smoked dramatically, just as he did everything else. He was a perfect O maker. He could make the rings in the air like a champion. I hated the way he smelled: the smell of an old ashtray mixed with too much Old Spice. I hated the discoloration in his teeth. His fingers were yellow. He was a hardcore smoker. In most photographs of him, he had a cigarette in hand.

I smoked my first cigarette when I was eighteen. Until then, I was always grossed out by smoking. I smoked because I had a lifetime of stress and I was hungry. I was in a bad place when I was eighteen. I was living in my car, working a full-time job, and was signed up in college. I rarely made it to class. I was living on my own. It was a difficult time. I smoked to fill my stomach. It was the cheapest trip to the grocery store and was always reliable.

By the time I got married and had my family, I was a seasoned smoker, just like my dad. My choice in cigarettes were Marlboro Reds; at least they had a filter. Go big or go home! I had to get my teeth cleaned more often than most people. I rarely wore a French manicure for fear of it turning yellow. A person's eyes and fingernails will always tell you if they smoke, how much they smoke, and how long they've been smoking. I smoked throughout my pregnancy and feel like someone should shoot me for doing that. My habit was intense. I only do things full throttle. In my gut, I knew my marriage was a fraud. This knowledge was killing me. I just didn't know how *much* of a fraud it was. I kept on going and plowing through life with my best friend—a pack of Marlboro Reds.

Over the years, I tried many times to quit. I used patches, pills, creams, etc. I maybe made it one full day with these aides. I used to lay in bed and say I felt weak. I used to claim my arms felt limp every time I tried to quit. How dramatic can one woman be?

By the my father finally died, he'd had various heart attacks. I saw the evidence of what the Pall Mall had done to him over a lifetime. It was disgusting. In the hospital, I watched as they drained the phlegm from his body. The visual of this should have been enough to quit instantaneously. Instead, I ran downstairs to smoke. My father knew I was a smoker, but I never smoked in front of him. I never wanted him to feel that he had passed this habit on to me, although he did. I didn't get the blue eyes, but I got the nastiest habit ever! I'm lucky!

My father died the year my son was born. Three years after that, I learned my marriage was a fraud. The smoking reached E.P.D. levels. I was a chain-smoker. I was spending thousands of dollars on cigarettes annually. I could've bought a small house with all of the money I spent trying to die.

In the year 2010, my ex-husband flew me to Los Angeles to meet Kerry Gaynor. A mutual friend of ours, Rene Garcia, had successfully quit using the Kerry Gaynor Method. His son-in-law, Alex Pirez, had recommended this to me. I AM GRATEFUL! DEEPLY GRATEFUL!

I spent three days with Kerry, and I quit immediately. No patches, crutches, or bullshit. I handed my last carton of Reds to a man in Beverly Hills who thought I was Vanna White, and I never looked back. I was a nonsmoker. I did it! For eight and a half years, I was able to breathe, live, and feel like a nonsmoker. No one could believe it! I had a hard time believing it.

The Kerry Gaynor Method is magic. I spread the news like wildfire. I helped Andrew Shack, my friend in California, promote this magic. I had the need to help others like me. It worked. I'm a cheerleader for all good things.

This method works. Kerry taught me things about myself that I never knew. Thank you, Kerry and Andrew.

Two years ago, I began dating one of the baby loves that I briefly mention in the "I am a lover" chapter. He doesn't deserve his name mentioned. He cheated, and I don't promote cheaters. It killed me. I grabbed a cigarette at the Swan restaurant in the Design District in Miami and inhaled deeply. I cried. I choked. I was back. The death wish was back. Pharrell wouldn't be happy about this. Ironically, Alex Pirez and Pharrell own Swan, the place where I fell into smoking again.

I called Andrew in California and confessed. He encouraged me to stop immediately. I disobeyed. I've been smoking for two years now. The baby love was the trigger, but the foolish choice was mine and mine alone.

I signed the final agreement last week with my ex-husband and pray that the attack of close to ten years is over now. I am preparing to quit again and stop the death wish once and for all.

Smoking is gross. Smoking doesn't discriminate, and neither does stage four cancer. I fully understand that my next cigarette could be my last one. I didn't come out unscathed from my divorce or from my upbringing. I have a few bad habits. I am human. I bleed just like you. Wish me luck on this one—this habit might be the most difficult abusive relationship I've ever been in.

Secret: Nicotine is out of your system in twenty-four hours. There is no such thing as failure or addiction.

CHAPTER 16

i am resilient.

I twirled the baton as a child. My two ponytails were always lopsided, and my smile was always the biggest. I twirl on a pole like a stripper does at E11even. I'm much shorter than your average stripper and use the pole for core strength more than any other reason. I swing the Steel Mace like a man in a gym—the Steel Mace and I have become one. It's a tool that mimics the spine. I am, by popular opinion, an extraordinarily strong woman that has always been interested in dominating what is unusual. If anyone can have it, I don't want it. I have never been attracted to common exercise. I am not attracted to anything common. If it is unconventional, strange, and unique, I want it. Rare is sexy.

I remember when my ex-husband stood in front of me and said, "You are not going out dressed like that." It was the first time as an adult woman that I remember thinking, "Oh no you didn't!" He can cheat on me. He can steal from me. He can lie to me. But I will roll over dead before he tells me what I can and cannot wear.

My father taught me to be a loyal, obedient, and serving wife. I did that. He never said, "Listen to his fashion rules."

I laughed silently and slipped out the back door dressed exactly as I was. I was on my way to a televised spin class at MCycle, the most popular spin studio in South Miami at the time. The television coverage would hopefully bring fitness into others' lives. I am a certified spinner on two levels. I was wearing a zebra print training bra and leggings. Animal print is swag. This time, my ponytail was perfectly curated and my smile was the biggest. What had I done wrong?

My love for adult fitness began when my son turned ten. I was always physically active as a child. I was highly competitive for all my life. I have Scoliosis in an S shape and am short. I wore a fiber glass back brace for six years. This was always a disadvantage. I worked harder to compete at everything. I was a fast runner, but my form was less than pretty. I was a cheerleader in high school. The cheer squad at the Bethany Hills School in Bethany, Canada was very well dressed. It was a boarding school for girls. I played goalie for the soccer team, they chose me because I was loud. I was a gymnast, a ballerina, a dancer. Being heard is my specialty. My life was an active life. But as an adult, my ONLY activity became my family. The Magda I once was became a memory, fading every day. It was fine by me. I was married to the man I worshipped and had a conventional family. Family was my highest goal.

It was my son's tenth birthday. I threw him so many over-the-top birthdays. Celebrating my child was particularly important to me because I had no one to celebrate me. This birthday party was at the MCycle spin studio. I thought it would be nice to include the parents in the birthday activities. Burnie the mascot from the Miami Heat joined—he's always good for creating hype. A good chunk of the New York Yankees came. I was close to Laura Posada, Jorge Posada's wife, and he also brings an enormous amount of spirit. Our children were friends at Gulliver Schools.

It was a circus. It always was. I adored celebrating my son. I enjoyed it more than he did. It was me making up for my lost childhood through him. My son, Roman, is not as social as I am. I like that about him. I thought it would be a great idea to have the children spin and the mothers join, and the fathers watch the other mothers. It was a classic Miami community event. I was known for having big birthday parties for my son; event planning is fun for me.

What I did not bargain for on this day was falling in love with fitness as an adult. I had no idea my life was going to change drastically and irrevocably, and it did indeed change at that birthday party. I met a lady named Maria, the spin instructor assigned to our party. She was a deeply passionate lesbian, a mother of two, and a catalyst in helping me see that I was living a lie. I am forever grateful to her for this.

She said, "Why don't you get on a bike?" I was confused. I was the hostess; I was the client. I was the mother of the birthday boy. How on God's green earth was I going to sweat profusely in my matching coordinated birthday outfit just to get some exercise? Roman and I always matched on his birthdays. I am extra.

Something inside of me was awoken. She tapped into the competitive, active Magda. I thought that Magda had died. But no, she was there in there somewhere, and Maria woke her up. I acquiesced to her request, as there were photographers all over the place and I didn't want to look like a scaredy cat. I mounted a bike. How hard could it be? I stayed on the bike for a few songs, flashed the @REVETE smile and hurt like a motherfucker. I could not walk for days. I could barely sit on the toilet. I did not let anyone see that. I did not share that with anyone. I knew it. I felt it. I was humiliated. I am a top producer, first at everything. Why couldn't I walk? What the fuck happened to me on that bike?

Her one simple question changed me for life. She dared me to live. She dared me to be me again. She woke up a beast.

I had been, for most of my marriage, a physically lazy woman. We did not exercise. We ate out almost three times daily. We were gluttons. I love to cook, but he never encouraged home cooking. I was a smoker. I was very unhealthy. I stopped caring about myself. I was overweight, lethargic, and, in a way, depressed. I was not happy with what I had become. My friends from Toronto were perplexed, too. I was only vibrant and energetic for Roman. The rest of me had become invisible.

I was always a pretty girl, but you could tell that I had become a small version of MAGDA. I could tell. As a young girl, I took a lot of pride in the way I looked, and throughout the marriage I just stopped caring. *He* stopped caring. I love makeup. I love to dress up. I stopped doing that.

When that spin instructor asked me to get on the bike, she professed the rest of my life. She was Walter Mercado.

I got on the bike and I never got off. Riding that bike was transformational. It became an obsession for me. It also became a lifeline. Every stroke of the pedal became hope. Every song I sang out loud became future. I was alive again. I understand how this seems cliché. It is not. After decades of abandoning myself, this simple physical activity gave me the space to remember I mattered too. It was meditation. Meditation is a great place to find yourself. I had lost myself. I meditate daily now. It is all in the habits, EVERYTHING is in the habits.

I will always be grateful to that spin instructor. Her momentary presence changed my life forever.

If you ask anyone that personally knows me, they will confirm that I am CERTIFIED in all things gym. I mean, EVERYTHING.

I do not like claiming things that are not mine. If I tell you I am a hula hoop champion, I am. If I tell you I am a yoga teacher, I am. I am not a fan of saying you are something you are not. If you are an accountant, do not pretend to be a CPA. Pretending to be something you are not is NOT for me. I am more of a "take me as I am, or don't!" type. It is especially important to me to get all the education I possibly can. I skated through high school because God is good. I have a GED. The confusion of different education systems in Canada and U.S.A. almost stopped me from walking into college.

I did not graduate from college. I wish I could have had parents that helped me through the college process. I always wanted to be an attorney—an attorney that would help women and the less fortunate. I sold my soul to get my son into college. I have more student loans than doctors do, but he is the best credit risk I will ever know. I was an unsupervised child. I did the best I could considering the tools I was afforded. Therefore, I am thirsty to learn, thirsty to grow, thirsty to improve, and there's always room for improvement. When you stop wanting to be better, I think that is when you die. Healthy things grow.

After dominating the bike, the ride, the return to me, I realized there was more. Thank God there was more.

I got hungry for more. And then I became certified in this and that and this and that. I became certified in everything to do with fitness. I am a one-man gym. And what's interesting is I still have so much to learn because fitness never stops. I am not the most fit woman in the world. I love to eat rich, decadent foods. I love to drink delicious red wine and DON JULIO 70. I love to smoke Marlboro Reds.

That is not fitness, it is truth. It is balance. Tell the truth and shame the devil! Fitness is knowing thyself and being thyself. If you abstain from the bad, you cannot understand the good. I am a realist. I love balance. For the most part, I am a healthy eater Monday through Friday. On weekends, I live hard. I wake up in the dark and practice the habit (that word again) of taking vitamins and supplements, a variety of collagens and powders, doing fasted cardio (HATED IT) and lifting weights daily. God knows there are mornings where I say, "Why am I doing this to myself, why am I waking up at this Godforsaken hour?" It is just insanity. It is my lifestyle. The most insane, difficult, beautiful, rewarding, painstaking lifestyle. The best part of this lifestyle is its loyalty. It is the most allegiant. It never betrays you. It never cheats on you. I LIKE THAT A LOT. There is nothing more glorious than investing in something, anything, and reaping the reward, getting exactly what you put in.

Ideally, that was what marriage was going to be like for me, too. I put in everything I had into my marriage, hoping I would get everything back in return. That was not the case in my marriage because that had to do with another human being and his harem. In this world, the only human you can control is YOU!

Fitness became my crutch. My body transformed, my mind became strong, and my will to be HAPPY took a victorious breath again. With my new body came an enormous amount of attention from my peers, fellow fitness enthusiasts, old friends, and my family.

The new and improved me was not celebrated by everyone. The people around me that I believed were cheering for me were not. My ex-husband was one of those people pretending to be happy for me. He was not.

I think it scared them. It scared *him*. They did not support me in this journey, and I didn't give a shit. My son supported me in this journey, and he is the only person I need approval from. I realized the attention I was getting was superficial. I never really thought of myself as a fitness guru, but that is what I became. I became a source of information for both men and women. I was inspiring people I knew and people I did not. I went the extra mile, and I became certified in things that usually women do not do. Like Austin, Texas, I like to keep it weird. Some of these practices included the steel mace, the club bells, kettlebells, and pole dancing. My yoga practice is hugely different than traditional yoga. I like to keep my practices strong, farfetched, and unconventional. Why not be the best in everything you possibly can be?

Of course, I have been approached by many people to open gyms and make money from this, but that was never of interest to me. Surviving was my goal. Using fitness as a tool to build a better life was my finish line. I do not want to be a slave to a fitness business. As an entrepreneur, as the owner of the accounting firm together with my ex-husband, I knew well what ownership meant. It is a never-ending responsibility. One of the habits (that word) I learned was to compartmentalize. I love fitness. I would never jeopardize that because of business potential. I love marriage, I would never jeopardize that because of temptation. You feel me?

Running a fitness business is slavery. My idea was to be a slave to my family. God laughs at people with ideas! Family was my wish; running a business was never my goal. My goal now is just to be the best I can be. Fitness has taught me a lot about this practice. This practice NEVER stops, never abandons, never lies. Like numbers, it does not lie.

It is exponential truth. The older I get, the more I want to learn the new and different fitness techniques offered. I do not want to run full marathons anymore. I am an accomplished runner if you ever saw me run, you would die laughing.

I have awkward form. Like Phoebe from *Friends*.

I have run all over the United States with a former Guinness World Record holder.

While I was running, I would ask myself, "What the fuck are you doing right now? Why are you doing this?" The pain in my shins was horrible. The pain in my lower back was excruciating, but I needed to cross the finish line every time. It was important to me to accomplish marathon running, just like it was important to me to become certified in everything. I didn't need guidance from my parents for this education. I didn't need approval from my husband for this education. All I needed was me.

I am a yoga teacher at a local studio in Wynwood, Florida. It is the first time I accepted a public paid job as any type of fitness instructor. I am a coach, and now paid for one-on-one sessions. I am having the time of my life teaching classes and empowering humanity. I love when I get new students and have the privilege of introducing them to something that I know is revolutionary. I will never forget the fitness teachers and students in my life. They all had a hand in resurrecting the strong, confident MAGDA I once knew and loved.

There are so many differences between fitness practitioner and fitness teacher. It is incredible. Knowing something and applying it is the greatest challenge for most. But I am a teacher. I am a master life coach. I am a cheerleader, and I am a practitioner. The combination has served me well. It has helped me survive the horrible debacles in my life. I believe that fitness is something that I inspire in many people. I am close to fifty years old. I stopped caring about a man loving me. I began to love myself. I have abs. I have the little boxes on my stomach people pay for. My trainer Grant Weeditz and I always laugh about the boxes, every box I get is almost like a tattoo. It's almost like every peak and valley on my body, every mark, every line, every indentation tells a story. They remind me of the parts of my life that I want to forget, and some I'll never forget. Maybe I shouldn't forget them, because they keep me humble. Everything happens for a reason. The memories and boxes on my abdomen keep me stable. They keep me real. Fitness is not a class. Fitness is not a certification. Fitness is not a membership. Fitness is something you are every single day.

I go to sleep at the exciting hour of 9:30pm every night. I predominantly wake up at about 5:00am every morning. I wear my sunglasses at night. I have rituals. Mine are different from yours—we are two different human bodies. I am thinking about launching a platform. A platform that incorporates my fitness, my coaching and the media world all together: the thrilling @REVETE life is a rich blend. My sister Mimi created one for yoga, and she is truly inspiring. If I created a platform for me, would you subscribe? Also, have you followed me yet?

On this platform, I would talk about fitness. Not body bullshit, not boxes, not the superficial part. It would be about the holistic approach to fitness. Being fit is never not eating a chocolate bar again. Sometimes being fit is escaping domestic violence or loving yourself when no one else does. This would be my focus on my platform. Whadya think? The genius that edited this book loves this idea.

Being fit is doing the best you can in your life with your resources, every day. That is what it is. That is what fitness is.

I cannot say that I am the same as Mark Megna, a former NFL player I know and love. Or the same as Ray Allen. Or even the same as my trainer, Grant, because I am not. And I never will be. Nor do I aspire to be. I am not the same age, gender, or height. We do not have the same genes. We all have one thing in common: we are all fit. Fitness has no owner, no prototype.

Fitness is about discipline and commitment. It is about wanting to cross the finish line.

I needed to mentally cross the line. Whether it was ugly, appropriate, expensive, painful—it did not matter. Fitness has been a tool for me that just sits there, a tool that patiently waits for you. A tool that does not hinder. A tool that does not encumber. A tool that does not manipulate. Fitness is a tool for me to survive. It is so patient. I use this tool once a day, at least an hour minimum, but sometimes, I use this tool four or five hours a day. When I have issues or problems, or I get sad, chances are, you are going to find me in the practicing of the HABIT of fitness. Chances are, you are going to see me eating healthy. This is the tool I use to overcome, and it has served me well. It is faithful. It is loyal. It is the sexiest forever after I have ever experienced. It is timeless, like my favorite singer Barbra Streisand.

I am not someone that you should imitate when speaking of fitness, that would be unrealistic. If you have not figured it out yet, I am an extremist. I am someone that can guide, motivate and educate ANYONE on what fitness can do in their life.

I am an unusually relentless fighter; I fight even if it hurts. I suppose this is why I hang out with MMA fighters—I understand them. I will continue to move forward. Most people give up. And that is the part I want to inspire in you, like the spin instructor inspired in me. Pay it forward. Tap into your beast. Fight your demons. Find your tools.

Never give up. Never stop.

Keep going, even if it is painful. I am hoping my platform, my book, my media, my pain moves you. And if not, I am online. Ever since COVID-19, I have been doing online sessions for everything. You got REV! I am approachable. I will not bite you; I reserve those actions only for ex-husbands. If you want to explore yoga with me and see all I offer, check out my website, www.atreve-t.com, and let's play. My yoga practice is aggressive. You have been warned.

Mind over matter is my key. Major key! When people ask me how I ran all those marathons, I reply that it was easy. My mind leads me, my heart follows, and my body is my vessel. On my first marathon, I ran 36.3 miles without any professional training at all. It was mind over matter—also, I was in love with my running partner. If I got through sitting in jail because I had a fist fight with a man, chances are, I am also going to get through a marathon, whether it's 36.3 miles or not. Nothing is ever going to stop me from meeting my goals. I could fail; I am human. But I do NOT believe in failure. I will keep trying until I succeed.

It is because I have that tool of fitness that failure doesn't exist. I own the catalyst of a strong foundation. Fitness is not about wearing a bikini. It is not that I do not give a shit about how I look in a bikini—it is just not my goal. My goal is about feeling strong, feeling ready for anything that life throws at me. Fitness has been a pseudo-church for me. I hope that if you do look to me for fitness inspiration, that you understand my fitness level and your fitness levels are different, that my practices and my rituals will always be different, that you should check with professionals in your area before any type of physical risk. I believe in acupuncture and I also believe in medicine. I am a ying and a yang. I am flexible. I am hungry for every type of betterment. I would like for you to take that desire from me. Imitate that.

That is the only real wish I have for you. This is the best advice I can give you in absolutely everything. GET HUNGRY!

I now have a hernia. It is in the center of my six pack. I laugh every time I see it; I call it my little ball. At least it's not a pearl. You must love the bad to appreciate the good.

Secret: I am still very self-conscious when wearing a bathing suit.

CHAPTER 17

i am heaven's DNA.

Hozier's "Take Me to Church" is one of my favorite songs. I see my life in episodes, and the church episode in my life is one of my favorites. And, exactly as Hozier says, I ended up worshipping like a dog. We can change in one day. I think this episode is the most uplifting.

For as long as I can remember, religion, for me, was always an enigma. We can fall in love in one day. I was a non-practicing Catholic born to a Cuban family. I practiced a little bit of Catholicism as a younger girl, and by the age of thirteen, religion was over. There was no more practicing religion. There were no more white lace dresses. ZIP! NADA! In Bethany Hills, we went to chapel. We sang, "OH THE LORD IS GOOD TO ME," but I did not *really* believe that. I did not believe the Lord had been good to me. I sang because I am a soprano and love to show off. Deep down, though, I thought the Lord forgot about Lil Rev.

The next time I was faced with religion was at my wedding. My dress was one hundred percent silk, and I wore an enormous diamond cross. It was an heirloom in my maternal family. My wedding was at a non-denominational church, one that permitted a divorced man to marry a never-married woman with no red tape. I followed protocol like a soldier, but religion remained dead to me. It carried no value, no substance.

The next time I was faced with religion was at my son's baptism. I duplicated what I knew. His baptism, his communion, and finally his confirmation took place. I am a dutiful mother. It carried little purpose. He will also be married one day and figure out his own religious path if that is his wish. I cannot wait to meet his wife. I, for the most part did not believe in a higher power. I had lost my way, my step and my faith many times in my life before. I was faithless.

I really lost all hope when I realized that my ex-husband was a cheater.

78

If there was a GOD, why did he let me trust him? Why did he allow me to place all my faith in him? Why was I violated as a child? Why wasn't I protected? Why didn't GOD protect me?

I gave up on God. I gave up on heaven. I gave up on faith. I chose to never practice any type of religion again. A little after my divorce, maybe two years after, I began dating a Jewish man younger than I was. (I can make Kugel now. I speak a little Hebrew.) His family practiced religion, and I did it with them. We would go to synagogue. We would practice Judaism. This piqued my interest because of the community. I thrive in community, and people of the Jewish faith have an extraordinarily strong community. I come alive in a team—ask anyone at Anatomy at 1220. I thought Judaism was beautiful. I decided to study this further. I wanted to learn more about this culture, this religion. I became extremely interested in it. I even considered converting as my relationship grew with my younger Jewish man. Maybe there is some truth to this stuff. Maybe there is a light, maybe there is a higher power guiding us through all of it. Is his name David?

My relationship fell apart and my study came to a complete halt. Once again, I was reminded that no faith can save us. I did not practice anything at all after that. I did not execute anything. I abandoned all religion again and continued practicing life. I was comfortable in life's practice. It is what I knew. I continued dedicating myself to parenting my son, working, earning, and working out. Those were my religious acts every single day, until I met Grant and Tiffany Weeditz.

We all have a voice, and we should all lift our voices. We should all tell our stories—we all have a story to tell. Grant and Tiffany showed me their story in action. They are truly religious. Church encourages us to do this. My cousin, Vanessa Borge, had also mentioned this church to me at one point, her opinion was a meaningful mental note.

The beginning of my faithful life was starting through my fitness workouts. AMEN! A miracle was in motion. God was reaching out to me through Grant and solidified the strong hold through Tiffany. In retrospect, God did not know what he was doing. @REVETE made it to church!! Call him God, Jesus, Lord, David—it does not really matter. *Someone* up there was calling me in. The only church I knew was my gym. The only GOD I referred to is my son. He was there protecting me. He is here protecting me now. How did that become this? That is the question that I do not think I will ever have an answer to. How did practicing life hardcore take me to church? I am talking about the basics. How did that become this?

There is a GOD.

In your life how does one thing become another? Think about it. It might be your miracle, bro. It might be that you are a miracle. It might be that something or someone is watching out for you. This is how it happened to me. I am heaven's DNA. I hear people say there is no heaven, there is no hell: there is only now. I do not agree with that. I used to agree with that when I was a faithless person. I do not agree with that anymore. I changed in one day. I think the older I get, the more I realize there must be a higher force working for us, through us, protecting us. I mean, it is a miracle. It is a miracle that I am not dead, considering the way I grew up. I should have been dead. I am *not* dead. I am alive and protected.

Was somebody speaking faith? Was there somebody protecting me? Are you there, GOD? It's me, MAGDA.

Throughout my younger life I felt like a reformed atheist. I did not speak this language. I remained silent.

I did not speak against faith. I remained silent.

Grant and Tiffany spoke faith to me. They did not remain silent.

They did not preach to me.

They did not say, "You are a sinner, Magda." They did not say, "If you don't go to church, you will grow a hunchback." Quite the contrary. They said, "Magda, life is better with church." It was my belief in them as human beings that got me to the starting line. It was trust. TRUST is the hardest for me to give.

I have run many marathons in my life. I never felt intimidated. And yet, I was terrified to go to church. I went by myself on the first try, and I was afraid of being recognized. I was afraid of being saved. I sat in the front row, alone, and cried. I clapped. I cried again.

Vous Church is a local church in Miami, Florida. It is a community. It is what I found so alluring in the Jewish faith: community. It is what I live at Anatomy at 1220 daily. IT IS STRONG. They do help everybody in our city. Yes, they collect donations, but not like Tammy Faye Baker did. I was shocked at its very relaxed environment. You can wear jeans to church. There is no judgement. There are plenty of drug addicts, cheaters, rock stars, and thieves in the audience. There are people. Church is people. They do not deny that. There are sinners, and they do not deny that, either. I am a sinner. You are a sinner. If you say you do not sin, you are lying to yourself. You are not lying to anybody else. I think walking up to that starting line that day at Vous Church made me stronger in many ways. The strength I was building was different from going to Anatomy at 1220. It made my mind stronger. It made my heart open. It made my belief in religion new.

Religious people are not people who walk around with a Bible or people who preach or people who say they are better or act as if they are always right. I do not ever want to be righteous. Church offers no absolute. I want to be kind. I want to be understanding. AMEN!

Going to Vous Church reminded me of these things. The funny thing about church is it does not need to be marketed. It is already marked. This chapter is not about indoctrination or convincing anyone of anything. It is about showing possibility. Anything is possible. One day can bend your life. You do not need to sell church; church is already there for you whenever you need it. You do not need to preach church. You just need to *be* church. Church is people. I am people. This church helped me to understand that even people like me—that are very fallible, that are very imperfect—can be religious. There are so many people that still do not believe I go to church. I am not here to convince anyone of my goodness, or my holiness. On the contrary, I want people to know of my weaknesses, my problems, and my humanity, because we are all the same. We are all the same, whether you practice that religion or this religion, whether you use rocks or crosses or stars. It does not matter. The second time I went to church, Grant and Tiffany and I were photographed.

Our image was on the big screen. I remember looking at myself saying, "Oh my God, I'm in church." There is a God! There has to be a GOD!.

I decided to invite my son to the church. I did not force him to attend. He always has autonomy in my home. No one should force religion on anyone, ever. WACKOS exist! I am sure you know some. I respect my son and knew he would try just for me. He did. He loved it.

My son is not a devout Christian and never will be. He is balanced. He is even-keeled. He is religious but not a fanatic. My son is a good human being who has the freedom to choose whatever religion he wants unencumbered and uninfluenced and not bullied. I went to jail protecting my son's freedom of choice regarding religion, and chances are, I would go to jail again doing that. It took me close to fifty years to find my religious harmony. Religion and church are people. People who need people.

That is all it is.

It's people being good to one another. It is faith. You do not need anything else. You do not need a book. You do not need to touch someone and cure them of their ailments. You do not need a guru. You do not need a preacher: what you need is firm and fearless faith.

My faith was restored. Thank you, Pastor Rich Wilkerson, Grant and Tiffany Weeditz, and cousin Vanessa for restoring my faith. The heavens spoke to me through you.

Who are your people? Name your people. Name your church. Give it a title. Go there every day. Find your church. Find your strength. Find your power. Walk fearlessly. Audit YO circle.

If you still cannot find religion, that is okay. I'm a yoga teacher. Look for my schedule and we will practice spirituality. I think they are two different things, but I think they are intertwined. It would be a loving NUDGE to your starting line.

Secret: I am on my knees at the shrine of life.

CHAPTER 18

i am lucky.

On Sundays, I usually listen to Barbra Streisand, play with my orchids, and drink healthy juices. This is a practice I developed at the wise old age of thirteen years old. I was a weird, unsupervised young girl. I developed some rare habits, and my love for Barbra was a premature and everlasting one. I learned to use Sunday as a restoration and preparation day for the coming week. I use my serious case of self-diagnosed O.C.D. as a tool. Today, I thought I would write the chapter "People who need people," which turned into "I am lucky." Barbra Streisand is my favorite singer in the world, and the song "People Who Need People" has always been extremely near and dear to my heart. I believe we are the people she sings of—all of us. I believe church is people, too. I believe we cannot make it through this life without people.

Usually, you think "the people" in your life should be your spouse, your family, your best friends, your neighbors. Unfortunately, in my life, too many people have murdered me time and time again. I had to look outside of the box to find my people. Those key people that pulled me through, carried me and loved me through all of it.

Some of the people that I am going to discuss in this chapter love adulation and love name recognition. Some do not like it at all. And what I love about these few people in my life is that they have gotten me through most of my life *because* of their differences, because of what makes them unique. The one trait they share, though, is that THEY ARE ALL FEIRCELY LOYAL. I think the only thing that they all have in common is their loyalty. They are all committed people. Commitment turns me on. I am electrified by this quality. They believe in faithful. They believe in fidelity. They believe in truth. I think that is one of the things that keeps me close to these people, always.

I can only entertain people that do not possess these qualities for an hour or if I am getting paid to do so.

I am going to start with my son. He is my purpose, my reason, my center. He is one of the people in my life that had to be there because, you know, children need money. This young man has been a constant reminder of unconditional love in my life. Always. He is honest. He is exclusive. There was a long time where I did not know why I had been born. Where I felt unwanted and unwelcomed in this world, and then, I met Roman. I met my purpose. One day he will be a great husband. I cannot wait to meet his wife. Until then, he is my number one fan, friend, and person. He is the most loyal of all the bunch. He has indeed become somebody I need, and this is not because he is my son. It is because he has earned his stripes. He is my best friend. He is a great roommate. He is a great ally; he is trustworthy. Hallelujah, I broke the mold. I am lost without this people, this person. ROMAN EMPIRE. I LOVE YOU.

There is a former NFL football player who has made serious touchdowns in my playbook. I never imagined a professional football player landing in my life, but he became a constant source of inspiration. He exemplifies discipline, commitment, and loyalty. He reminds me a lot of myself. We met about five years ago. I will never forget it. We had breakfast and we discussed a social event I was working in. He and I have been doing social events ever since. Moreover, we have collaborated in rearing my son, uplifting humans, and creating a better world.

He said something to me that breakfast that I will never forget. I do not even know if he remembers, but it really resonated with me. He said, "Magda, when my gate is open, everything comes in. But when that gate closes, it never opens again." I remember when he said that, I thought to myself, "This is someone I need and want in my life." It is kind of weird. Was this my brother?

He is a married man. He has a beautiful wife. She is my friend, too. It is always important to me to know and love the spouses of my friends. It is respectful. I think the reason I love talking to Marc is because he has wisdom. He reminds me that there are faithful men out there. He reminds me that there are people in this world who believe in goodness at all costs. Against all odds, he is a constant source of regimen, another trait I picked up during my unconventional life. I am not certain what they taught Marc Megna on all those fields and all those gyms or if he learned those lessons in Fall River, but Marc, I am so very grateful for what you learned on the field and what you learned from your mom, because it helped me. Thank you for being a constant source of resilience and leadership in my life.

I think I am turning Lebanese. I am not sure how it all happened but somehow, in Miami, I was able to land in the care of a Lebanese gang. Make no mistake, these people make the Cosa Nostra seem weak. There are many of them. It is a mafia. Family is something I was robbed of. My father was much older than my mother, the odds of a strong family vibration were slim due to this.

During the process of my life, I did gain a new family, and it is Lebanese. I speak a little Lebanese now. Just add it to the other five languages I speak.

It is beautiful how they came into my life. It is funny. It started through my son, and then it just grew. Healthy things grow. Now I have a whole legion of Lebanese family. Like Cubans, Lebanese people have suffered greatly. We have all suffered a lot. They bind together and remind me what family feels like. On holidays after my divorce, I used to celebrate alone with my son. I used to fight for creative ways to make his holidays healthy and happy, but with the Lebanese clan always backing us up, it has been much easier. I am incredibly grateful for them, all of them, even though half the time I do not understand what they are saying. I guess that is why we are so close. They are probably criticizing my pseudo-Lebanese accent.

Out of my Lebanese clan, Mimi is the heartbeat of this alliance for me and Roman. She is also a constant source of love and trust. She is younger than I am and currently going through some similar situations that I have already been through. I do all I can to help her in her journey. It is the least I can do. We are indeed adopted from Lebanon. Mimi was my neighbor, and maybe the only neighbor in my life. We traded food, company, and memories for years. This was new to me, and I love firsts. This really exuded the definition of neighbor. Mimi was my neighbor, will forever be my neighbor, and was one of the people that got me through the difficulties of my life. I am so grateful for my Hallas Yella.

Before I was Lebanese, I was Canadian. I speak French. Just add it to the other five languages I speak. The Cannucks, my Canadian family, are my constants. This family is led by my roommate and my son's godmother, Tarah. When I met Tarah, I was thirteen years old. A lot happened to me when I was thirteen. I did not expect Tarah to be in my life now that I'm forty-nine, but Tarah and I have been sisters throughout the entire ride. She was there when I met my husband. She knew Chris and liked him. She knew my rapist and did not like him. She was there when I had my son, her godson. I was there when she had her son. She was there for my dad's funeral. I was there for her dad's funeral. It's a sisterhood and a friendship that cannot be duplicated.

I am incredibly grateful for my sister Tarah. I moved to Miami and created a life, and our relationship was impervious to the distance. I didn't get to physically see her, but she remained a daily constant in my life through the computer, telephones, and social media. Our relationship grew stronger. I do not know how I would have made it without her. My Canadian family is made up of sisters. We grew up as sisters at the all-girls Bethany Hills School in Bethany—Dominique, Tessa, Ashlynn, Shannon and I had a family. We grew up together. These women are my family, and Tarah is my center.

There is a young girl who came into my life through my stepson Valy. She was beautiful. She has great big green eyes. She was a brilliant, straight-A student. I met her when she was about ten years old, and she is now a CPA at the firm my ex-husband and I built together side by side. She came into my life through divorce. She was the one who named my marketing agency @REVETE.

Her parents got divorced and it was a horrible situation. Divorce has a funny way of breaking things and making things, and this divorce made Natalie who she is today. I am incredibly grateful for that. The pain that she suffered, the pain that I watched her suffer, was the catalyst to her success. In this case, pain was her friend, just as pain has always been my bestie, too. I would like to think that I helped her through that pain. I wish someone would have helped me the way I helped her, but she helped me through mine as an adult. She is loyal as fuck. Natalie is like a daughter to me. I think when she owns her own firm, and has her own family, she will remember the life lessons that I taught her: not just the stuff that I taught her in the office, but the life lessons that I taught her in the process. She luckily has not had to apply those lessons yet, but she knows them. Knowing lessons and applying lessons are two quite different things.

Natalie has been a constant source of love and loyalty and wisdom in my life. I have had the luck of finding wisdom in so many different faces, so many different humans. This young girl is one of them. If you ever need a CPA in the future, ask me, I will proudly refer you to a little girl named Natalie. She will always be part of my legacy.

Lynette is one of those people that does not like adulation. She is a shy woman.

Lynette became a friend of mine through my marriage, an asset I kept. I met her through my ex-husband. I introduced her to her current husband. I married them. Today, they are happily married. I think that that is indicative of the person that she is. She has also been a constant source of strength for me: she has betrayed the loyalty of protocol through marriage to remain my friend. She never sold her soul for a free tax return. That speaks volumes of Lynette and her integrity. Lynette is family, forever family.

I went from family to family to family. I learned language after language after language. This is the story of my life, people. The people in my life have gotten me through my entire life. Lynette is one of those people. I love you.

Liz does not want to be named in this book or anywhere else. She must be one of the most private people I have ever met. I love that. I share that with her. Believe it or not, for such a social media star and now author, I am a very private person. I would even classify myself as paranoid at times. I feel that Liz understands life in a different way, my way. This lady's long list of accolades is impressive. I am not going to go into them because she might disown me for doing it. Let us just say she owns a lot of International Emmy Awards.

She is an amazing human being. She has been a source of wisdom to me for many years. It is funny how loyalty is shown through action and sometimes inaction. Liz reveals loyalty every time. In time, Liz has shown me only love, strength, and good sense. Cheers to those that still have it—common sense. I think one of the best lessons she ever taught me was to surrender. It is a hard one. I am the yoga teacher, and here comes one of the best journalists in the U.S.A. teaching me to let go. I should understand the fundamentals of what that signifies better than she does, but my strong character always gets in the way. I am an inherent fighter. Liz has always taught me to let go. She says, "Stop fighting." I listen to those that are wiser than me. Liz, I love and respect you immensely.

Shannon Allen is her name. I can say her name because she is married to Ray Allen. Yes, Jesus Shuttlesworth. Being in the public eye is not even a choice for these people. But what is funny about these people is that they are only people—they are only human beings. We are all the same. When you are fortunate enough to meet someone like Shannon Allen and fortunate enough to be welcomed into her home and her family, then you fully understand that they are no longer celebrities, that they are just people. Kind, honest and loyal people.

I have had the blessing to have these people in my life for all the years of my son's schooling. We went to an incredibly special school in Miami, Florida. I say we because the parents had to graduate, too: we paid top dollar, but we were also in the fight. Gulliver Schools know how to teach and build family at the same time. Raiders for life. Shannon and I became friends working hard side by side at the school. She is not one of those mothers that are full of shit or delegate to others. She is a workhorse. Shannon has had my back throughout all my divorce, and I have had her back throughout all our Gulliver life. Since we met, I knew I was not alone. Nothing will ever change that.

My love for basketball did not grow because of my relationship with Shannon. My love of basketball was never affected. We are friends. She and her husband are those key people. I love them. They remind me every day that cohesiveness is urgent. They remind me of how faith is necessary, and how hard work is a plain daily fact. I love you, Shannon.

She is going to kill me for saying her name. She is a lot like Liz, very private. She is very elegant and highly organized. Toni has been a very loyal friend since the kids met. Her children also went to Gulliver Schools. Gulliver Schools has been a blessing in many ways. I believe it was the constant my son needed to get through the separation of his parents, and it was a place for me to make long-lasting relationships. After I left Toronto, I thought I would never form long-lasting relationships again. Man, was I ever wrong! Gulliver Schools introduced me to many wonderful men and women. One of those wonderful women is Toni. (OOOH… she gonna murder me!)

Toni is a source of innocence for me. She reminds me of what I was like when I was married, always trying to survive dutifully. The process of divorce and feeling lost is so challenging. Feeling like a pawn in a game of money, business, and relationships is like running an endless rat maze. A marvelous mother, she reminds me of what motherhood should be. And we have that in common: our skills on mothering are remarkably similar. She is a hover disc and so am I. I love you, Toni. Thank you for being a constant source of safety for me.

In my life I have met many men, many strong men. A good example is Peter Miller, a three-time World Sail Fish Champion and also a parent from Gulliver Schools. We ended up being great friends. He is another celebrity in my life who will not mind me saying his name. Why? Because he has a TV show. It is okay to sing the accolades of TV celebrities.

I have met extraordinary men. Another is a young man named Grant Weeditz. Grant came into my life maybe five years ago when I was forty-four years old. Grant became not only my friend, but kind of like my son. I do not think his mother would like me saying that because he has a wonderful mom. I do not care: I love him like a son, and he became a constant daily source of clean eyes for me. He is consistent. He is honest, just like Roman. He is inspiration for me. He does not lie. He does not cheat. He does not steal. He is a rare breed.

He does not like it when you talk about him in this form. He is very modest; I would even say he is bashful. However, he looks like a monster, a huge block of muscle. The bigger they are, the harder they fall, and he fell for a wonderful lady named Tiffany who also became my family. His wife became my little sister, another constant source of honesty, loyalty, and faithfulness. The Weeditzes introduced me to Vous Church in Miami, Florida.

You must understand my views on religion were not good when I met the Weeditzes: they were nonexistent. They took me to this church pretty much by the hand and led me to the door. I did not understand what the purpose was. They did not want me to swim in a tub and become baptized. They did not want me to pledge money. They just wanted me to find hope and strength and faith, and this is precisely what happened. I am still shocked that that happened. I am still shocked that my trust in them was so deep. I remember walking into church reluctantly and in a negative mindset.

My hesitance was overcome by the voice of Rich Wilkerson. It is because of Grant and Tiffany and their love for me that they were able to not influence me but *inspire* me to take the time to open my heart and meet faith again. When I met Rich Wilkerson, I fully understood what they meant.

Rich Wilkerson is a preacher. He does speak for money. He does speak on a stage. He does collect money from the church. Does that make him a bad person? This makes him a hardworking income earner that does good.

For most of my life I was an atheist. I was born and raised a non-practicing Catholic. How I ended up in front of Rich Wilkerson is a miracle in motion. Rich Wilkerson becoming one of the people that gets me through life was simply amazing. It was Grant, then Tiffany, then born-again faith.

There have been many times, in Rich's care, that I have raised my hand in church on a Sunday standing next to the Weeditzes and yelled like a mad woman at an Elvis concert. This place restored my faith. Rich Wilkerson has given me strength in many ways that are foreign. I owe it all to Grant and Tiffany.

They became family members. They go to all my celebrations. I go to theirs. They help me move. I help them move. This is called "People Who Need People." I love them, all three of them.

Finally, the last two people that I need to mention are currently the most important. They are my biggest protectors. They are both prominent businessmen in Miami. They are faithful to their families. They do not cheat, steal, or lie. I was on my last leg when I met them. I was alone and could not trust anyone. My ten-year divorce wiped me out, emotionally and financially.

The reason these two men come into my life was purely serendipitous. I was referred to them by one of the Communist Terrorist's biggest haters. She's got a lot of haters. You reap what you sow. The problem with hurting innocent people is KARMA! Steve and Phil are the ONLY two men who were able to take all the abuse that I suffered from in the never-ending *Kramer vs Kramer* saga, and they honestly protected me.

These two men stood together side by side and defended me. They did not shy away from the mess my previous lawyers left. They did not shy away from the phone calls made to judges. They did not shy away from the Communist Terrorist attorney beating me up daily and excessively.

Litigation is not fun. CPAs and family attorneys in Miami come a dime a dozen, and the honest ones are rare. These two men saved my life. I cannot scream this loud enough. They are superheroes. They illustrated goodness, truth, and integrity every step of the way.

Phil Shechter is a forensic CPA in the State of Florida and an Iron Man. Steve Nullman of Nullman Law is my God. My savior.

I am still in the process of litigation and fear being sued again. Please know that I am always willing to discuss ALL the names involved in my divorce if it helps another human avoid the pain and abuse I endured through this process.

If you ever have the good fortune of meeting Steve or Phil, thank them again from me. They deserve every mention in every article, in every magazine, and on every microphone I ever touch for the rest of time.

Barbra Streisand and I go way back. We met when I was thirteen. She knows me well. She knew I needed people back then and every day thereafter. I am so fucking happy to celebrate the people in this chapter.

Secret: The strongest people in the world are the most needy.

CHAPTER 19

i am open.

I created my most recent vision board at Toni's home on December 31, 2019. This is how we welcomed 2020. I sat with Toni on the private beach at Soho House in the final months of 2019 and we charted out the map of this book, the blueprint. A new blueprint. She is a professional home organizer. She is my organization guru. Maria who? On the vision board are all my hopes and dreams for this year, and every year of my life, really. I am faithful in all things, visions included.

I sold my house at a small financial loss this year. My realtor was court-appointed. She is the worst human being ever. I had little choice in this matter; it was part of the omnibus of abuse I suffered post-divorce. I moved out and am incredibly happy in my new home. I look at the dolphins swimming in the ocean daily. I saw myself writing this book with this view many years ago.

I kept the vision board through the move. It is in my new bedroom. My new beau, Ron, promised me it would all come true, my visions. I am not sure if he remembers saying that to me. My heart skipped a beat when he did. And he was correct: they all did. He was on the board, too. I just did not know it was him at the time. We created our 2021 vision boards together. I am in love with him. Cross your fingers.

On the board is this book, my life. This book is my life. My life without social media, without my parents, without fear. I had a desperate need to tell everyone I am imperfect. I am a GED holder, a self-diagnosed O.C.D. haver, and a smoker again. I have been writing this book since I was thirteen years old.

A lot happened to me when I was thirteen. I have been wanting to ask for help since then, too.

Asking for help is a craft more people should explore. I have been longing to help others since then, too.

I have always been a philanthropist. I have been promoting everything I love since then, too.

I have always been a cheerleader on the radio. I have been a stellar performance since then, too.

I have always been an overachiever. This book is a long-term vision. I am a long-term goal crusher.

I HAVE NEVER BEEN AN AUTHOR. Wish me luck.

On the night we created the boards that wonderful New Year's Eve, I was going to try to quit smoking again. Isn't that funny? Plan and God laughs at you.

I am still in litigation. I hope that this will end in 2021—Steve and Phil are all over that. But so is the Communist Terrorist working against me. Wish me a lot of luck.

This book will consume most of my 2021 year as I am planning a media takeover to tell my story. I own a marketing firm and am over-the-moon thrilled by the idea of being my own client. Magda working for Magda! Now do you get it. My story had to be told. It is my harnessed O.C.D. working miracles in my favor. Do you have a story to tell?

I am turning fifty years old in ten months and I have one more bucket list item pending. This too is on the board. Fiji, here I come. I do not really change my visions often. I just add new ones. I am LOYAL to a fault.

I trusted the wrong human beings. We all have. I stopped relying on myself to make my visions a reality. Big mistake. Check your circle.

My vision board included the color red. It did *not* include declaring bankruptcy. Yes, I am in the red. After having been to jail, fighting off a Communist Terrorist for a decade, losing my marriage, and having a healthy and successful son, I suppose paperwork and financial regrouping should be a walk in the park. I will let you know in my next book.

I also used the red to remind me to leave a mark on this world and to keep it sexy. In all things, keep it sexy. It was my turn to share my real story. When you are in court, you cannot speak. You cannot decide. You are at the mercy of what you pray is an arena without prejudice—BULLSHIT. In life, it is inappropriate to say everything you want to say. I believe they call this diplomacy. I am not diplomatic, and neither is John Mayer. I chose red almost as a dare. I wanted to dare myself to look and feel the best I possibly could example: fitness, nutrition, Miami Social Media representation, podcast. I have a reputation to protect, after all. I am @REVETE.

I travelled a lot this year. That, too, was on the board. Hopefully, I will travel more to meet you, the reader of my life. The future owners of my story. I have no real ties to Miami, Florida now. My son is well on his way to conquering his own world. Travel is in my future. Maybe relocation. Anything is possible.

This book began as a cry for help from an unsupervised child decades ago. I can still find my teenage chapters in old photographs. It then turned into an angry account of all the wrongdoings I had suffered in my twenty-year BURNING BED movie.

I hope this book ends up being an uplifting place, something anyone can read, something that shows we are all the same. We are human. We are all looking for love in all the wrong places. We are looking for things in too many faces. We should only look to ourselves to realize our visions. It is in knowing thy true self and in being thy true self that we can crush all our visions. BTW, I am a Certified Master Life Coach. Is there anything left about me you do not know? Follow, follow, follow @revete.

The excerpts of my life that I included in this book are chosen with great purpose. Each painful, joyful, and out-of-left-field memory was written with intent. I do everything with deep intention. It was my intention to elevate you. It was my intention to make you laugh till you cried. It was my intention to make you hope. It was my intention to find peace. That is my greatest hope.

Secret: I am now an author! BAM!!! Who are you?

foreword.

The definition of surrender is to yield power, control, or possession of another upon compulsion or demand... to give oneself over to something.

With this book Magda has surrendered and made way for her future.

May the honesty of her journey help us all learn to let go.

Liz

transitive verb

1a: to yield to the power, control, or possession of another upon compulsion or demand

surrendered the fort

b: to give up completely or agree to forgo especially in favor of another

2a: to give (oneself) up into the power of another especially as a prisoner

b: to give (oneself) over to something (such as an influence)